TEN WORDS THAT WILL CHANGE YOUR LIFE

Barbara H Hayes Ph.D
310 274-0218

Ten Words that will Change Your Life

ERVIN SEALE

 DeVorss *Publications*

Originally published by William Morrow and Co., New York

First DeVorss & Company Edition, 1992

ISBN: 0-87516-651-2

DeVorss & Company, Publisher
P.O. Box 550
Marina del Rey, CA 90294

Printed in the United States of America

TO ELVA

P R E F A C E

ONE OF MY MOST POPULAR private classes had to do with the Ten Commandments. This book contains material used in that class. I offer it now as an introduction to the study of the Bible for our times, and as a basic manual in practical metaphysics.

In this book I have not gone into detail on the subjects of prayer, mental health, healing or on the demonstration of their techniques and formulae. The careful reader, however, will not miss the fact that these are nevertheless precisely the burden of the book. Understanding of the Ten Commandments will give one power in prayer. Power in prayer will give one all else. With the Great Law as rule and guide, every human problem can be solved.

"Now go, write it before them in a table, and note it in a book . . ." (Isaiah 30:8)

"I have written these words. . . . I write them in a book in order to write them straightway in my soul, and receive in my mind the imprints of a script more divine and ineffaceable." (Philo of Alexandria)

"I have not made my book more than my book has made me." (Montaigne)

THE TEN

I. I am the Lord thy God, which have brought thee
out of the land of Egypt, out of the house of bondage. Thou shalt have no other gods before me.

II. Thou shalt not make unto thee any graven image,
or any likeness of any thing that is in heaven above,
or that is in the earth beneath, or that is in the
water under the earth: thou shalt not bow down
thyself to them, nor serve them: for I the Lord thy
God am a jealous God, visiting the iniquity of the
fathers upon the children unto the third and fourth
generation of them that hate me; and shewing
mercy unto thousands of them that love me, and
keep my commandments.

III. Thou shalt not take the name of the Lord thy God
in vain; for the Lord will not hold him guiltless
that taketh his name in vain.

IV. Remember the sabbath day, to keep it holy. Six
days shalt thou labour, and do all thy work: but the
seventh day is the sabbath of the Lord thy God: in
it thou shalt not do any work, thou, nor thy son, nor
thy daughter, thy manservant, nor thy maidservant,

COMMANDMENTS

nor thy cattle, nor thy stranger that is within thy gates: for in six days the Lord made heaven and earth, the sea, and all that in them is, and rested the seventh day: wherefore the Lord blessed the sabbath day, and hallowed it.

V. Honour thy father and thy mother: that thy days may be long upon the land which the Lord thy God giveth thee.

VI. Thou shalt not kill.

VII. Thou shalt not commit adultery.

VIII. Thou shalt not steal.

IX. Thou shalt not bear false witness against thy neighbour.

X. Thou shalt not covet thy neighbour's house, thou shalt not covet thy neighbour's wife, nor his manservant, nor his maidservant, nor his ox, nor his ass, nor any thing that is thy neighbour's. (Exodus 20:2-17 Authorized Version)

INTRODUCTION

THE TEN WORDS WHICH ARE THE GREAT LAW

THE BIBLE CONTAINS THE SECRETS OF LIFE and shows the way to health and happiness, and while it is there for all of us to read, all of us may not always understand. This book is to help you to understand the Bible, to provide the key that will unlock its pages and show you how its wisdom can be invaluable in your life. The Ten Commandments form the heart of the Old Testament, and the foundation of the New. They are, indeed, a summation of the significance of the whole Bible. The Bible itself is the concentration of thousands of years of man's meditating and thinking upon the ways of life. The Commandments are, in turn, a concentration of that vast wisdom arranged under ten heads, affording a clear, simple pattern for the eager young mind as well as an outline for study by the most profound thinker.

One of the prime requisites of every person's life is the

knowledge that, as the saying goes, he can write his own ticket in this world. The most practical and profitable kind of knowledge a person can acquire is that knowledge of his own spiritual resources which can equip him to handle the daily problems of living. From this comes a great and heartening assurance that there is always something that can be done about every problem, and that no man is ever without hope or without resources. No situation of pain or trouble should be tolerated for very long in any individual life. Through constructive thinking and scientific prayer, every individual can do something about every situation, and make things better and nearer to the heart's desire. But this assurance and this security and strength will never come from viewing the Bible only in the traditional way, nor in reading the Ten Commandments as a mere series of prohibitions and restraints upon human conduct.

The Ten Commandments, or the Ten Words as the ancients also called them, comprise the Great Law which was handed down by God on a mountaintop in two tablets of stone. This is a figurative way of saying that the Law descended from the highest level to our plane where it remained stable, fixed and abiding. The fact that it is divided into two parts is equally significant, for thus does it reflect the pattern of division in all things in nature. There is the spiritual and the material, the subjective and objective, inside and outside, active and passive. This equal division of two tablets, each bearing five commandments, is no accident and was not, as some commentators have lightly suggested, contrived out of a love of numerical symmetry. The tablets are an implicit recognition of the dual nature of man. *God created man in his own image,* but *male and female created he them.* That is, man is two, and these two are the expression of the unity that is God.

The first five commandments all refer to the spiritual world, or the world of thought and consciousness. They deal with causes. The first five commandments are a scientific prescription for constructive right thinking. The second five commandents refer to the objective side of life or to man's outer actions, to his relationship with objective things and other men. The arrangement of the Ten Words is implicit recognition of the law of action and reaction upon the mental plane. The Bible takes it as axiomatic that all external action is the result of internal thought and it suggests that if one gets his thought right, his action inevitably will be right. Thus the first five commandments are all concerned with getting the individual thought correct. The second five commandments describe how that thought works out on the external plane of life in harmony with all things and with all men.

The two tablets are like the two pages of an open book on which are written the basic truths men live by, but the real book is man himself. The study of the Ten Commandments, then, is only a study of ourselves, an endeavor to read the language of our own nature. For man is a book which is sealed. All the life of man is a conscious or unconscious attempt to break the seals and read the wisdom imprisoned within. Every man is only the record

of thoughts which have been inscribed upon him by his
own thinking. One side of man is thought, and the other
side is action. All of our lives we hear two voices: one, the
voice of hope and desire which rises like a fountain from
within us, and the other, the voice of fear and doubt and
hesitation which comes from without. Fear and doubt
seem stronger than hope, especially in our early years, and
the marks they leave on the easily impressed minds of
childhood are deep. This we discover when at last we try
to know ourselves and read what has been written into
our natures. Then it is that we find that fixed thoughts
and old habits impede our action, and we find that two
parts of ourselves are in battle.

To everything on earth there is an inside and an outside. The person who does not see and understand this is
in conflict with the side he does not see. Like Jacob of old,
he fights with an invisible being who is both enemy and
angel. For example, when a man quarrels in his mind
with the material world, or with any material fact or situation, and finds it offensive, or cruel, or a hindrance to
him, he is guilty of imperfect vision and of an inner imbalance. He is trying to ignore everything but spiritual
values; he is, as we say, "in the clouds." His idealism
which rises from within is quarreling with the conditions
he sees without. With proper understanding there should
be no quarrel because physical conditions should not oppose the ideal within.

On the other hand, the person who tends to accept facts
as the only reality, to minimize the intangibles, to consider

spiritual ideas as having little practical reality in this world, is more or less out of touch with the causative world. Engrossed in things, he is oblivious to the causes of things. Since he will not use ideas, ideas will use him, and they may in time become an enemy to him. Everyone has to come to terms with his adversary: one must understand, reconcile and harmonize the warring part. A spiritual workman is not used by any pair of opposites; he uses them. The basic, daily quarrel in human life is the quarrel between desire and immediate environment. A man wants to earn more money, but he is in a rut with an old job. A girl wants a husband, but cannot meet the right man. A business man yearns for peace of mind, but his affairs keep him in ferment. In each case, the inside quarrels with the outside.

The Bible teaches how to resolve these conflicts. The Great Law lays down the basic rules and formulae. It says in effect that desire is of God, the ideal is from God, and has a dynamic, creative potential. The facts of environment should not obstruct desire, but rather be responsive and cooperative. The mind that sees this and operates upon this basis will change facts and fulfill desire and realize its ideal. The means of doing this is true prayer.

In prayer the mind writes upon its own impressionable surface. In ancient times the men who knew the law were called scribes. This was in observance of the truth that every man by his own thoughts becomes his own lawmaker, formulating day by day through his thinking the opinions and conceptions which will become the statutes of his life.

When by repeated thinking he establishes a certain opinion or concept in the subconscious which is then mixed with emotion, this concept becomes a force directing his outer actions. This is the great law of action and reaction on the psychological plane of life. Whoever sees this can be said to have been initiated into the kingdom of heaven because it is the first step toward a life of self-government. By constant reference to the Great Law, he will make his thinking more constructive and thus legislate for himself new freedom and happiness. Every man is strongly urged to look at these undying tablets of the law as demonstrated in nature and make a duplicate of them in his heart. "He shall write him a copy of this law in a book . . . and it shall be with him, and he shall read therein all the days of his life . . ." (Deuteronomy 17:18-20) In other words, every person who looks into the principles of his own nature and finds the natural law of God written there shall make his own thinking and acting conform to the principles of things. Learning to write, in the divine sense, he will be able to write a new chapter in his life. When man can read the divine words and principles and understand them, he can then reproduce their action on the scale of his own individual life. Thus, his personal life and all its activities become his copy of the eternal book.

Of course the Bible and the Ten Commandments are big enough to be read on several levels. They take into account all types of understanding and all degrees of consciousness. Those people who are not yet aware of the ways of their own being and therefore cannot live by the inner spiritual law, have to live by outer laws and regulations. They will read the Ten Commandments simply as a series of edicts from a superior power, formulated to provide the rules for their conduct. But the person who has gone beyond this level of thinking, who has discovered the power within himself, has also accepted the spiritual responsibility for his own actions. He will then see the Ten Commandments not as restraints upon his conduct but as prescriptions for his thinking. This is the spiritual understanding of the Ten Commandments; it is also a scientific understanding, because it can be applied in daily life. It is with this spiritual and scientific view of the Great Law that we are most concerned.

Most of the world's problems today are problems in human relations. Success in business, politics, and even in international affairs, depends more and more on the ability of each man to understand his fellow and to get on with him. Each man's psychology determines how he will act. If he is angry inside, his speech and behavior will show it. If he is disappointed or discouraged, his relations with other men will be discouraging. Thought governs fact: mood determines action: mind is matter and consciousness is fate. If you want to get along with your neighbor, get along with your God or with your own thoughts. If you want to have peace and happiness in your external life, you have to build peace and happiness in your thought.

The two tablets of the Ten Commandments provided for this long ago. One side plainly depends upon the other. You cannot benefit from reading one side without knowing the other. The first five commandments, on the left-hand side, are careful instructions on how to keep your inside nature in order. This is primary and fundamental. Right action follows right thinking as automatically as a chemical reaction follows the proper preparation of the ingredients. In modern metaphysical study or scientific right thinking, a man is always taught to get his thoughts straight first and let the action be born out of the thought. Never treat conditions or people as things that can be changed or manipulated by external means alone. Rather, if you want to change any condition, you must first recast your own thoughts about it.

Because the sense of reality in so many of us is projected outward, we have to make laws and write them in books and read them from courtroom benches. These laws impress us more or less and so regulate our conduct on earth. But, as everyone knows, they are not wholly adequate. A law that is written down in a book or upon a stone, however sacred and revered, can never compel a person's obedience if that person's consciousness is in conflict with the statement of the law. This is borne out by the whole history of the human race. No law ever written has yet prevented man from making a fool of himself. There is not a law upon our statute books that has not been disobeyed at some time by some person. The Ten Commandments are the foundation of all modern law. Everything on our statute books is in some way a variation of these ten basic rules for living. All our civil law is but a representation or a poor facsimile of the divine law. The civil law is absolutely necessary and right for a society which is in ignorance of the spiritual law. Men tend to believe that the laws of their lives come from without and not from within. And so we have laws, but the point is that outside regulations for the conduct of man have never really improved that conduct. It may be shocking to hear, but before you finish this book you may well realize that there is not one of the Ten Commandments which has not at some time been disobeyed by every one of us. The commandments and all their variations and additions in the modern civil code are broken every day and have been broken continuously since the beginning of civilization upon the face of the earth.

There is a legend which illustrates this nicely. When Woodrow Wilson went to heaven, he was a disappointed, discouraged and frustrated man. He had drafted fourteen points for world peace and had poured out his soul in the endeavor to bring peace to the peoples of the world. In heaven he sat upon a park bench in the Elysian fields, holding his head in his hands, bemoaning his lot and deploring the attitudes of certain people on earth. Along came Moses and seeing Mr. Wilson in this sad state of mind, inquired, "Why, what's the matter, Mr. Wilson?" Mr. Wilson replied, "Just look what they did to my fourteen points." Whereupon Moses answered, "Oh, come now, don't be so downhearted. Look what they did to my ten!"

Rules and prohibitions are for children and they will

always be broken. It doesn't seem possible to bring up a child without a certain amount of rules, regulations, threats and cajolings. As the eight-year-old said to his grandmother after he put on his mittens and his hat and coat and his rubbers, "All right, Grandma, give me my don'ts." A child does not reason from within, so parents and teachers have to reason for him. A child may grow tall and pass the age of twenty-one but still remain a child in certain matters, and still need his prohibitions, his don'ts and his shall nots. A mature citizen, on the other hand, has long ago discovered the reason for the laws of society and knows that they were made not to restrain him in his liberty but to protect his liberty. The law is always for the citizen, not against him. The traffic light placed at the intersection is not put there as a hindrance but as a protection. If there is no traffic light at a busy intersection of life, the mature man will use his innate caution and discretion and live and conduct himself according to the inner law of his own wisdom.

Just as there is a positive reason underlying every civil law, so is there positive teaching behind each of the divine commandments, and knowledge of this teaching will bring the earnest student one day to the glory of God in his own being, and to freedom and happiness in his external world.

The truth of being is that every man is a law unto himself. Every man's thought is the law guiding his experience. The one who does not know this is in ignorance. His ignorance is projected outward and demands that a law be imposed from outside to tell him what to do and what not to do. Thus man, who is by nature free, becomes a slave to his own unknowing. The moral law with its don'ts and its musts, the rules and regulations of church, society and state come in as disciplines for the minds which cannot discipline themselves.

The natural law is the Great Law, the wisdom inherent in the Ten Words. The story of how the Ten Commandments came to be makes this evident. The original tablets, we are told, were the work of God. "And he gave unto Moses, when he had made an end of communing with him upon mount Sinai, two tables of testimony, tables of stone, written with the finger of God." (Exodus 31:18) "And Moses turned, and went down from the mount, and the two tables of testimony were in his hand: the tables were written on both their sides; on the one side and on the other were they written. And the tables were the work of God, and the writing was the writing of God, graven upon the tables." (Exodus 32:15, 16)

In the spiritual history of man, Moses represents the subjective side of mankind. He is the man of God who receives the tablets of the law directly from God, which is a way of saying that man receives the law directly into his nature. The tablets are written both on the inside and on the outside, which is to say that the law is in our whole being, in our thought and in our action, in our inner spirit and in our outer world, and both are one.

There is a legend that says that the first tablets were made of sapphire, formed of the divine breath and holy dew. They gave forth the eternal verities in letters of fire,

but the idolatrous people could not understand the meaning of the flames. So the second set was hewn by Moses out
of rough stone, but gave only temporal truths or a shadow
of the real. Legends, of course, are illustrations of psychological truths and have their basis in reality. Spirit is a
living fire and within its sapphire radiance are the holy
laws of man's being. Ordinary understanding which deals
with the material world and considers it the only reality,
cannot see this. Hence the people could not make use of
the original tablets, for those who do not or cannot see
that their outer world is a reflection of their inner states,
must perforce have a cruder version of the Great Law.

We read in our Bibles that Moses, the man of God,
came down from the mountain and saw the people engaged in worship of idols, of worldly goods and ornaments,
and unable to devote themselves to the laws of the spirit.
Disappointed and angry, he broke the original tablets and
went back to the mountain to ask God what to do. Thus,
in the beginning, man could not accept the tablets of the
law as God sent them down to him. To go back for a
minute to the symbolism of the legend, his immature
understanding could not stand the brilliance of the sapphire. The light that lighteth every man that cometh into
the world was too strong for his feeble eyes. So the original tablets were broken, and a substitute pair given to
man. It is the substitute pair which we read in the Bible.

The Bible is the great textbook on man's freedom, and
the Ten Words are an epitome of all that it says. They
symbolize, at the same time, the nature of man. The two

tablets representing the conscious and subconscious, or the subjective and objective side of man, are together the Book of the Law. There must be thought before there can be action. If you look carefully at the first five of the Ten Words, you will see that they refer to man's relationship with God, that is, to the inner world of thought. God is our term for the spiritual being, for the ruling force of the realm of the nonmaterial. Each commandment which defines our true relationship with God is setting forth the law of constructive thinking. Once understand the meaning of the first five, and you will have no difficulty with the second five. The two sides are as closely related as cause and effect, thinking and practice. Psychologically speaking, one side is consciousness and the other its manifestations. Just as God keeps his agreement according to the contractual relationship with his people set up by the covenant, so will knowledge of the truth lead to success.

The Bible is the spiritual history of all men and of any man. After it speaks of the Ten Commandments, it speaks of the ark of the covenant in which the Law, or the Ten Commandments, was placed and carried about by the children of Israel. The ark of the covenant is a term for man himself. Man is the carrier of the Law. His law is in his heart. Moses advises us not to seek the word, or the cause of misery and happiness, in any height or depth, because he says, "The word is nigh unto thee, even in thy mouth." Man points his telescopes toward heaven to study the composition and nature of the stars. He descends into the depth of earth and sea for treasures. But only when he descends into himself or seeks the spirit within him, does he discover the secret word which heals and saves. Knowledge of physics and chemistry changes the earth; knowledge of spiritual psychology changes man. Who will be so bold in today's world as to maintain that science of matter is more important than science of the spirit? As an ancient preacher in Jerusalem once declared, "All the labour of man is for his mouth and yet the appetite is not filled." We spend billions every year for research in all matters save into that of the spiritual nature of man himself. That continues largely to remain in the hands of religious doctrine, and in the domain of dogma and superstition.

In the ark of the covenant was deposited the Law or the Testimony. The Bible says that the ark of the covenant had two cherubim on its top side, with their wings stretched toward the center and just touching over and above what is called the mercy seat. These mythical and mystical creatures stand for the two parts of consciousness. Where their wings touch is the place where thought and feeling marry each other and generate a new state of consciousness and a new episode in experience. If you have ever watched the two carbons in a carbon arc lamp approach each other and the arc of white fire jump from one to the other until there glowed that intense white light that only a carbon arc lamp can give, you will have an illustration of what is meant by the mystical contact of quivering wings. Where they touch, God electrifies man and changes him. In the Bible this mystery of creation is spoken of as the descent of the spirit or glory of God between the quivering wings of the cherubim to touch man on the mercy seat. "There I will meet with thee, and I will commune with thee from above the mercy seat, from between the two cherubim which are upon the ark of the testimony, of all things which I will give thee in commandment unto the children of Israel." (Exodus 25:22) If you find within yourself the emotional response for your desire, the Spirit is descending, and between the wings of the cherubim God is meeting man upon the mercy seat.

The left side of the great Book of the Law is called the Law, and the right side is called the Prophets. The reason will be apparent to anyone who ponders the nature of the two sides as we have explained them. What you do inside is the law to your outside. This law is absolute and incontrovertible. The right side of the book represents your speech and action. What you say is dictated always by what you have thought. A new thought makes a new world but only when the thought engages the subconscious power. In modern times Freud pointed out that when we attempt to say something other than our thought, the subconscious short-circuits our conscious effort and forces us to voice our real thought. Slips of the tongue are indicative and significant. As with our speech, so our acts are dictated by our thoughts, by the thought patterns. Man's behavior is largely a result of conditioned reflex action. The term *conditioned reflex* came out of the famous ex-

periments with dogs made by the renowned Russian physi-
ologist, Ivan Pavlov.

Everyone knows that when you place meat or any food
before a dog when it is hungry, its mouth waters. The
glands of the mouth begin to pour out saliva in anticipa-
tion of the food. Pavlov qualified or conditioned this function in the dog. Each time he fed the dog he rang a bell.
He did this over and over again until the dog's consciousness came to associate eating with the ringing of the bell.
Thereafter Pavlov rang the bell without providing food,
whereupon the dog's mouth would water and the saliva
would flow. The dog had been conditioned to expect food
when he heard the bell and his reflexes functioned accordingly. Hence, the conditioned reflex. It is a short step
from these experiments with dogs to the conclusion that
man, too, is governed by conditioned reflexes. When he
acts, he does not always act with intelligence, out of conscious choice, but is compelled to act from within, from
some subconscious pattern that has been built inside of
him in all the years of his past. A person's nervousness at
forty or at fifty may be directly traced to quarrels and
tensions in the home when he was a boy.

Some have seen in the Pavlovian experiments a way to
recondition our whole society, to change the behavior of
an entire race. Modern Russian psychologists under the
Soviet influence see in Pavlov's results the conclusion that
ideas and emotions are merely conditioned reflexes of the
nervous system and that what we call mind is only a reactive mechanism. The truth is, however, that most of our

responses are conditioned in the mind, and without the mind no conditioned response could ever be achieved. It is only through the mind that the mechanisms of the body can be re-educated. The great value of the Pavlovian experiments was not in that they had proved anything new, but that they were another confirmation of an old, old truth, long ago seen and demonstrated by minds the world over. None has come closer in stating this truth than Solomon in his three-thousand-year-old statement, "As a man thinketh in his heart, so is he." (Proverbs)

About sixty-six years before Pavlov, a man by the name of Phineas Parkhurst Quimby was experimenting in an entirely different field, that of mesmerism of human beings. He observed and proved, as he put it, that "man acts as he is acted upon." He showed that man is acted upon by ideas and opinions and beliefs, and the conditioned response is always in terms of these ideas and opinions.

It has been said that man is perhaps just a mass of flesh into which emotional patterns are planted, so to speak, and that intellect has nothing to do with the formation of our habits and patterns. Indeed, the intellect has nothing to do with it, if by intellect we mean just cerebration or the conscious act of thinking and reasoning. But mind is more than intellect. Before the mind has learned to reason it is receptive to impressions from other minds in its environment.

"Our atmospheres mingle," said Quimby, and this explains how fears and anxieties as well as faith and assurance are transmitted from mind to mind. All children are imitators aping the actions of their elders and responding like fine recording machines to the emotional transmissions of people around them. Every mind is like a super-sensitive microphone picking up all the sounds within its immediate area. Certain sounds are repeated often enough, like Pavlov's bells, until they become emotional compulsions and dictate the functions of the outer man.

A child reared by a tyrannical father, for example, will often show in adulthood a nervous tremor which he cannot control. Childhood is long ago forgotten, but the record persists in the consciousness. When present-day circumstances ring the bell right, the record starts to play and the emotional dictator shouts his orders to the flesh to tremble and perspire, even though there is no earthly reason for it. We are all bundles of walking habits, fashioned from our own thinking and the thinking of others.

But it must not be supposed as is often the case with conditioned reflex theorists that we humans are the helpless victims of our training. Environment does do things to us. But what environment does is always subject to change. A woman of fifty has stomach knots and indigestion because her father was usually angry and pounded the table at mealtime. A man of sixty still suffers from asthma because in his precocious youth he developed the habit of getting by without honest work. A gambler and promoter of fabulous deals, he has actually never been more than a step ahead of the sheriff. He has been running all his life. He has never sat down to take a real breath of air. He does not know how it feels to sit quietly and breathe deeply.

But the father of the girl and the precocious nature of the boy are not the real causes of the present-day troubles of these so-called adults. Those are only the secondary causes. To dwell upon these secondary causes as fundamental is to get lost in a materialism from whose prison only the knowledge of the Great Law will deliver us. There is only one way to activate the flesh and that is through the mind. If the body becomes the victim of bad habits such as asthma and a nervous stomach it is because the mind has first been impressed with some suggestion of fear or anxiety and these suggestions are repeated over and over until a subconscious pattern is engraved. One cannot plead innocence nor take feeble refuge in that sniveling excuse of modern times: "I am not responsible; my parents did it to me." If a child grows up and is educated, part of that growing up and part of that education is a working knowledge of the spiritual law of his being. We have the Ten Commandments before us. We have Moses, the Prophets and Jesus. The Truth, gleaned from the meditations and experience of thousands of years of living is here. If the scientific Truth behind religion has become the victim of fanatics and creeds, then it is our duty to free the prisoner and let her (the Truth) enter into life with us.

Your bad habits and your sickness patterns, which were conditioned into you while you were in a state of unknowing, can be reversed, changed or obliterated entirely when you come to a state of knowing. When you do not know and therefore do not think intelligently, then things, conditions and other people think in you. When you understand the principle that "man acts as he is acted upon" you will begin the motions of your self-delivery from bondage. You will write your own ticket and make your own law according to the principle laid down in the Ten Words. It is some kind of thinking on your part which establishes all conditioned reflexes, either volitional thinking or involuntary thinking. In involuntary thinking, something other than your own intelligent will thinks in you and you become the unwilling victim of its hypnotic spell. Don't be afraid. No one ever went another's way who had a well-defined way of his own. This is a scientific truth easily proved to the most doubting mind. A full vessel cannot take any more. A house that is occupied will not invite tramps and intruders. Therefore, see that your vessel is filled with the water of life, see that your house of the mind is occupied with the best residents, the finest insights and perceptions. The process by which this is accomplished is nothing else than that which in religious thought is called prayer. Prayer is the great reconditioner of the mind and redeemer of the body, the one sure way man has of delivering himself from any conditioned reflex and establishing a higher mode of action.

This truth the Ten Commandments recognizes in its arrangement of the two sides of the Book of the Law, and in the nature of the words inscribed thereon. As the inside of a man is forever dictating to the outside, so the inside or first tablet is called the Law. It is the ruler and the governor of the man himself. As the outside or functional side of a person is always responding to the inside or the consciousness, so this tablet which represents the outside is called the Prophets. In the Bible a prophet always speaks for God, the creative cause. In ourselves it is the body, and all the outside function of ourselves, which speaks for mind, the creative cause. All action is revealed thought. "There is nothing hid that shall not be revealed." For him who can read, each of us is telling secrets as he goes. Thus all of our speech and all of our actions are like voices of the prophets proclaiming what God, the creative mind and the forming power within, has spoken as the Law from the mountaintop.

The Decalogue, as the Ten Words or the Ten Commandments are called, is a concise handbook on the mental law. The Ten Words are a summary of what the Bible has to stay. Later we shall see that these Ten Words are actually one word which the Bible reveals again and again from beginning to end. For the present, let us look more closely at each of the ten.

one power not 2

> I AM THE LORD THY GOD, WHICH HAVE
> BROUGHT THEE OUT OF THE LAND OF
> EGYPT, OUT OF THE HOUSE OF BONDAGE.
> THOU SHALT HAVE NO OTHER GODS
> BEFORE ME.

THIS FIRST WORD IS IN TWO SENTENCES. Literally speaking, only the second sentence is a commandment. From the standpoint of its psychological and spiritual meaning, *thou shalt have no other Gods before me* should be included with the Second Word or what is commonly known as the Second Commandment. We shall deal with it from that standpoint and in this chapter we shall discuss *I am the Lord thy God* as the central truth upon which all of the Commandments are based. It is a pronouncement designed to focus the attention of the mind at that point of concentration where power and right action begin.

It is useless to try to command or direct any power until we first acquaint ourselves with the nature of the power and learn how it works. This must be supremely true of that spiritual power which "runs the whole creation through." Can a man control his own actions? If he cannot, then it is useless to command him. If he can, then he ought to learn why, and how it is made possible. Counting this as the First of the Ten Divine Words, we shall observe that the others are elaborations and explanations. The First Word is a summary of the whole ten. It is like the foundation of a building: the whole superstructure depends upon it.

The First Word gives personal enfranchisement. It raises man to a higher plane and reveals in him the source of power and strength for his daily needs. It reduces a man's fears, gets the world out of his hair, takes the burden off his shoulders and enables him to make progress constructively and happily. It is a call to that mind, which is wandering in the wilderness of matter and haunted by the terrors of this world, to come home, to return to center, to behold the truth, to see the power "in the midst of thee." What the First Word says in a nutshell is this: Every man has what it takes. Every person born into this life comes equipped with a spiritual power adequate to his needs and purposes, no matter how formidable the difficulties of his position. There is a way out of every trouble. There is a way in to every good. A way out of trouble and difficulty is what most people are seeking. Egypt is the place of our suffering and difficulty and we would all like to leave it. Of course Egypt is not merely a geographical locality even in the Bible's account. Egypt is a state of mind or consciousness. It is found anywhere and every-

where in this world, on all continents and in all places. It
is a rich land, but not in the sense in which the Valley of
the Nile is rich in nature's produce. This mental land of
Egypt in which most of the world's population lives, in
which we all live at times, is rich in products of the mind.
It is full of ideas and opinions, creeds, imagery, descriptions of sights and sounds all related by the various sense
perceptions. These bear in upon the mind and often op-
press it.

Thus Egypt is a place of slavery. It is a land of many
gods. The individual finds himself ridden by one worry
after another and shunted from one anxiety to another
until he no longer has any peace or stability in his world.
His mind is the victim of his circumstances and his environment is ruling him. No mind can properly and
healthfully consider too many things at one time. In life
as in baseball it is extremely important to return to home
base at frequent intervals. Otherwise there is no score, nor
is there any fun. When the outside world dictates too
much what you shall think about, you are at the mercy of
events; the demands and vexations of your job boss you
around all day. The evening headlines bid you worry
about the mounting world tensions. A member of the
family is sick. And a host of other emergencies and irri-
tants demand attention from your mind. There is no
peace in Egypt, nor is there any freedom. You are being
rolled around by events and conditions, like a piece of
mud on the rim of a fast-moving wheel. You are not in
control of your situation. Your motion is not your own.

If the mud could move to the center of the wheel it would find peace, for the hub of the fast-moving wheel is still. Obviously the mud cannot do this, but you can do this because you are man.

If the mud could reach the center of the wheel it would find stillness indeed. But when you move to the center of your wheel or the wheel of life, you will not only find stillness and peace, but you will find power and capacity and the means of initiating movement itself. This is the burden of the Bible's instruction. Cling to the center, is the meaning of the First Commandment. No man will find peace until he discovers the power of his own mind to act upon conditions rather than allowing the conditions to act upon him.

There is only one power, says the Bible, and it is mental and spiritual. Things and conditions have no power in and of themselves to initiate movement in any individual, save insofar as they gain that individual's attention. The power is in the individual's mind and not in the things themselves. Worry exists only in the mind. Since the mind can travel, it need not remain with the things that distress it, but can move to its point of rest in the center of the circle. This traveling of the mind is prayer, and only the person practised in scientific prayer will know the supremacy of his own mind over the conditions of his life. To pray scientifically one must have a clear understanding of the mental law as stated in the First Commandment.

The First Word says quite plainly that mind or consciousness can bring us out of Egypt or out of suffering.

It says that whenever we come out of any difficulty or out
of any slavery or any distressing situation, it is this mind
or consciousness which brings us out. There can be no
experience without mind, and when mind changes, experience changes. Therefore, the road out of difficulty is
through a change of mind. The expression *I am* is a name
for inner consciousness or awareness. It is a description of
the basic nature of man. It is the announcement of his
condition of being. The term *I am* is a recognition that
consciousness or the function of mind precedes all manifestation.

A good way to understand how this principle works is
to think of yourself as you are a split second before you
awaken in the morning out of a dreamless sleep. For you
at that precise instant there is no world of form or shape
or color or sound. There are no buildings. There are no
people. There is nothing. Then consciousness returns
and the whole world is there again. Consciousness has re-
created the buildings, the people, the forms, the shapes,
the colors and the sounds. This basic state of being of
your nature, or this capacity to be aware, has created all
that there is in the world of your experience. To a sleeping man there is no world. To a man under anesthesia
there is no world.

In experimental hypnotism there are many good illustrations of the principle of mind-action. For example, in
the trance state a subject will see and hear and smell and
taste only what the operator describes to his mind. The
image seen by the operator's mind will be transferred to

the mind or consciousness of the subject and be seen or experienced by him. The subject can be told to go and take a seat in a chair which already has an occupant, but to the subject there is no experience or sensation save what has been described to his mind. He will take a seat upon the lap of a person already sitting in the chair, and though he appears to the spectators to be in an awkward position, it will seem to him that he is simply sitting in a chair by himself.

This is one example of the truth that what a man knows, he is, and what he is aware of, he expresses and experiences. The recognition of this principle will release man from a thousand illusions and usher him into a thousand joys. According to your belief, so it is being continually done unto you by the forces of life. Change your belief and you will change your experience. Maintain your conviction and no change in matter, no social change on the outside or any manipulation of conditions or circumstances will change your experience. This principle is the absolute Lord and sovereign of our life here on earth. The First Commandment would have everybody recognize this basic principle of being, and make it the center of his meditation.

The Bible is realistic and scientific in its approach to life. It recognizes the Supreme Being as a central unity and an infinite power. But it very quickly recognizes also that it is useless for finite minds to try to understand the complete nature of this Being from their limited points of view. "Canst thou by searching find out God? canst thou find out the Almighty unto perfection? It is as high as heaven; what canst thou do? deeper than hell; what canst thou know?" So speaks the Book of Job. (Job 11:7-8)

In other words, there is a cosmic power working on a cosmic scale and responsible for all that is. About that cosmic power a finite and limited mind can know little or nothing, but about that cosmic power at the point where it becomes and is man, something can be known. We can look at our own nature and see what makes us tick. We can examine our actions and reactions and discover the principles and laws of our being. A man like Edison, for example, does not stop to question the inherent nature of electricity. Mr. Edison is reported to have replied to a woman who asked him to explain what electricity is, "Madam, electricity is. Use it."

The Bible deals likewise with its concepts. It does not burden itself with long theological or mystical dissertations upon an unknowable something. It goes on the assumption that God has placed the secrets of creation within each and every one of his manifested parts and it is good sense for a man to look at the part and find his revelation there. The Bible does not deal with absolutes. It deals with what is before us and takes man as he is. Man is more than flesh and blood. He is soul. He is spirit. You are not just what can be pointed to with the finger. You are actually an unseen being. No one has ever really seen you, the real you, nor have you ever seen another human being. What is seen when any of us looks at another is only the form and garment of the spirit, but the real self is invisible always. This invisible self is known to us by inward senses which are not directly concerned with matter and its forms. This inner self is a presence which we have spoken of as *I am,* our sense and consciousness of being. In all of nature there are two sides to everything, an inside and an outside. This is true of man. The outside is body, form and action; the inside is consciousness (sensation, thought, feeling, presence, mind). This inside presence is divine because only divinity can create. Only divinity has the capacity to think and direct by thought the movements of material forms. Matter does not direct itself. Matter cannot impart movement to itself or to other matter. Matter is inert in this respect. Consciousness is self-moving and therefore eternal and divine, since it can never be deprived of its property. The external world has reality for us only while we are aware of it. It is our awareness that gives it its nature and quality in our experience. A stone cannot move itself but must depend upon some animate being or some force outside itself to move it. After the stone is set moving it is subject to other objects to stop its movement. In other words, it has no movement of its own and no capacity to initiate movement. When it receives a stimulus, it moves. When the energy is expended, it stops.

What is true of the stone is true of all material conditions and circumstances. They receive their motion or their movement from the mind of the person who is dealing with them. When this mind ceases to deal with them, they will lose whatever motion has been communicated to them. When the mind walks away from any problem, that problem will die and cease to exist for that mind. When a mind approaches any good desire in confidence, it gives life to that desire. Whatever receives its motion from another must die as soon as that motion is ended. That part of our being which does not depend upon motion or life from another source is independent and eternal. It is eternal because it persists always in its own nature and is never abandoned by its own properties. It is eternal, spiritual and divine. Lift your arm and look at your hand and flex your fingers. You have just witnessed an example of the self-moving power of your own mind. Your flesh is matter, made of the elements of this earth. They are held together by the animating power of your spirit. Your thought is the functioning of that spirit. When you thought to move your hand, it moved.

The phenomenal success of Sister Kenny's mode of treatment of paralysis victims lay in her ability to re-establish the mind's control over the paralyzed muscle. By working with the muscle and by speaking to the mind of the patient she was able to re-establish in that mind the conviction of its own ability to move the muscle. The property of self-motivation is peculiar to man's soul. The First Commandment would have you recognize this and live accordingly. From mineral through vegetable and animal to man we may follow the ascending steps of this principle in action. A plant is more self-moving than a stone. A dog more than a plant. And a man more than a dog. An animal must move within the range of his environment, but a man by the self-moving power of thought may change his environment and thus move more freely in a wider area.

From Cicero we have the record of a most remarkable dream of the second Scipio Africanus in which his father appeared to him and instructed him in matters of state-craft and war and finally about the indwelling divinity: "Everything that is moved by a foreign impulse is inani-mate, but that which is animate is impelled by an inward and peculiar principle of motion and in that consists the nature and property of the soul. Now if it alone of all things is self-motive, assuredly it never was originated and is eternal. Do thou therefore employ it in the noblest of pursuits."

To become aware of the sovereignty of consciousness over body and over environment is the great discovery. It is self-discovery and self-revelation. All things wait upon this in man and thus the First Commandment is a trumpet calling to man to bring back his wandering attention from the phenomena around him and to think upon the central truth of his being. To allow the mind to wander among phenomena and conditions is to tune in with the limita-tions of the world. For example, if you were in the middle of a particularly vexing set of problems, there is obviously little point in going around and around feverishly with the problems. The thing to do is to hold the mind still. You cannot do so as long as you concentrate on the con-ditions which move it to distraction. You have to have something bigger than you and your problem upon which to fasten your attention. This is the *I am.* It is bigger than all conditions, for it makes and unmakes conditions. Thinking upon the First Commandment and the law of self-motivation will start a new line of thought which you can apply to your problem. This will start a change in conditions. To make use of this law, as Scipio Africanus says, "in the noblest of pursuits" is to remember it constantly, to keep it ever in mind in all that you do, put it first in your thinking and acting. Keep in contact with this overriding fundamental and you will ever be at home in the great truth.

Thus the First Commandment is an instruction to remember, to recollect, to get in touch with the source and cause of things. The average person in trouble is too much like a baseball player who gets caught between bases. When the opponent gets too close, the thing to do is to seek the base. The base is the Lord.

What is the Lord? The Lord is the law. What is the law? The law is consciousness. What is consciousness? Consciousness is your thinking and your feeling and the reasoning behind such thinking and feeling. Then to get on base is to recall the spiritual cause of all action and experience. The spiritual cause is thinking and feeling. Break the oppression of the material world and your strength will return. Since thinking is cause, the condition is not cause. Therefore don't fear it. Retire to the stillness of your thought where nothing external can inhibit or obstruct; then you can think of new and better conditions. This is the ever practical import of the First Commandment. Keep on base in your thinking.

Antaeus in the Greek myth was strong only so long as he was in touch with his Mother Earth. When his opponent lifted him from the earth, his strength waned. The myth conveys the same psychological truth as the First Commandment. A man must have as a source of his strength something bigger than himself and keep in contact with it.

"I am the Lord thy God," says the First Commandment. This is a meaningful statement and extremely important to the understanding of the whole Bible. Our English Bible gives the impression that Lord and God and Lord-God are all to be understood in the same way. Not so with the ancient text. Lord is the name for the kingly power, the ruler and sovereign of life. God is the name for the kindly power. By Lord-God we understand the kindly power in full command. Not that these are actually different beings or different powers so much as they are different ways in which men approach the one power. We have seen that the divine power is sovereign. Nothing and no one gives it power. It is self-moving. It is the Lord of all matter or creation. To the person who does not know this power, it becomes a hard disciplinarian, a cruel master, much like a lord of the manor in the days of feudalism. The lord of the manor held the power of life and death over the serfs and to keep them servile in the hardest of circumstances was his business in life.

So to a person who does not know the spiritual law and his freedom therein, life is a hard taskmaster. The spir-

itual power is always Lord. It is the governing power.
But when one understands this power and works with it,
he becomes master of his life. God is thus the name for
the one power acting beneficently in a person's life. Whoever has some understanding of these principles will
readily see that the spiritual power is not only a Lord,
fierce and kingly, but he will perceive that this power is
good or God, because it inspires us with wisdom which we
cannot attain through the five senses. It strengthens us in
a way no food or medicine can ever do and it protects us
from misfortune with a wit and cunning beyond that of
the wisest man.

Lest the reader think I am speaking of a power foreign
to himself, let me remind him that these wonderful works
of God are done through the medium of man's own
thought. Mind is the divine agency on earth. It is the
only immaterial power we know. Your intuition, your
hunches and inspirations all come from the direction in
which you turn your thought. The burglar gets hunches
as well as the banker. The storyteller gets hunches concerning plots and characters. Each man's thought initiates
his action. If the thought is ill-considered, the action will
be ill-considered. A strong, confident train of thought will
restore the use of a muscle, change the rhythms and fluids
of the body and raise people from their sickbeds. A person of definite prayer practice conditions himself to a
higher kind of government. His God is no longer just a
Lord to be feared and wondered at. He sees that some
power is responsive to his directed thought, that it always

moves in the direction of his thought and that therefore if it is upward the power will take him upward. Thus, instead of experiencing the power as a coercive, chastising force, he feels it as a friend and guide. Instead of impersonal, it becomes personal. Hence, the meaning of the expression, "I am the Lord *thy* God." Lord means the Power, the Authority and the Sovereign Dominion of the Deity. A negative thinker will experience the reaction of The Power as correction and discipline or, as some call it, punishment. To such a person the Deity is a stern judge. A constructive thinker, on the other hand, will experience the reaction of the Divine Power as mercy and blessing and also as inspiration and energy. To this person the Deity is a Power and a Wisdom which authorizes good things in his life. It is the Lord *thy* God or The Power *thy* blessing.

If he has understood thus far, the reader will have discovered what it is that takes one out of bondage, out of Egypt, which, as we know, is the Old Testament's term for the bondage of the senses and the darkness of the mind in regard to true causation. Pain and hardship abide until this truth is known, the truth that consciousness is the directing cause of individual experience. We suffer pain and undergo privation until this truth is born in the mind. When it is so born and we know the single and first cause of our life's events, then we are free of all tyranny and may ascend into a freer atmosphere and a more pleasant environment. This is the meaning of the Bible's tale of Israel's leaving the overlordship of Pharaoh and trekking to the promised land. Moses is the subjective or inner nature of man and it is this that always leads. Another way of putting it is to say that your thinking is always leading you into your experience. "As a man thinketh in his heart so is he." Thinking in your heart is symbolized by Moses, your leader.

It takes a little while for a person to learn this law and to act upon it. Therefore this life is seen to be a school in which we are children learning to grow up into our spiritual maturity. In the beginning Moses rebels against the oppressions of Egypt and fights back against them angrily. This represents the immature condition of a man who fights with his environment and its problems. He is angry at conditions and at people and takes offensive action against them. For this reason Moses, the thinking nature of man, must flee into the desert of himself and there discover and meet with God in the wilderness. There he must come to grips with the spiritual truth of his own nature. There he must arrive at his own conviction and reach maturity and self-control in his thought and feeling. When this has been done the Lord will crown him with power, or give him power upon the earth. He will hear the voice of God saying within him, "Behold I have made thee god to Pharaoh."

This is one of the most remarkable statements of the whole Bible. It boldly says what a lot of timid people will be hesitant to believe, namely, that a man's mind or consciousness is God to his world or environment. As the sun in our heavens rules all life and expression upon this

planet, so consciousness or thought in man rules all experience in man's life. But as there is a sun which rules
our sun, and another sun which rules that, and so on into
infinity, so there are higher dimensions of the *I am*, the
Godly power, reaching into infinity. It is out of these infinite dimensions, it is out of these infinite realms of the
God-head that the voice comes to every man saying, "Behold I have made you God to Pharaoh" or to your world.

It's you no idols

THOU SHALT NOT MAKE UNTO THEE ANY
GRAVEN IMAGE, OR ANY LIKENESS OF
ANY THING THAT IS IN HEAVEN ABOVE,
OR THAT IS IN THE EARTH BENEATH,
OR THAT IS IN THE WATER UNDER
THE EARTH: THOU SHALT NOT BOW
DOWN THYSELF TO THEM, NOR SERVE
THEM: FOR I THE LORD THY GOD AM A
JEALOUS GOD, VISITING THE INIQUITY
OF THE FATHERS UPON THE CHILDREN
UNTO THE THIRD AND FOURTH GENERATION
OF THEM THAT HATE ME; AND SHEWING
MERCY UNTO THOUSANDS OF THEM
THAT LOVE ME, AND KEEP MY COM-
MANDMENTS.

NO MAN CAN SERVE TWO MASTERS. You cannot be loyal
to two propositions at the same time. You cannot say yes
and no in the same breath. You cannot expect fulfillment
of a desire if at the same time you frustrate that desire.
You cannot, that is, and avoid conflict. You cannot work

with your ideal if you acknowledge a barrier to it. The great psychological truth of man's mind is that the spirit of man must move as a unity. In this it will imitate the nature of the Great Spirit which is unity. Unity is a mathematical necessity. There cannot be two creators, for one would cancel out the other. The law of the spirit is oneness. The Great Spirit creates the universe and is individualized as man. Individual and universal are poles of the same being. Therefore, the spirit of man operates by the same rule and law as the spirit of the universe. When a man's spirit is divided within him into a striving after an ideal, on the one hand, and fear of barriers, on the other, then his strength is also divided. He goes in neither direction but stands still and wears himself out. This is the sin of man and also his suffering. There is no trouble in man's experience that does not come from this inner psychological division. Failure to see the truth of the first commandment creates this division and establishes a tendency to set up false gods.

What is a false god? Any god is an idea, a fact, an image or theory to which you ascribe the power of affecting you above your will. That is, it has power beyond your own. When you give any such concept power, your own power leaves you. Thus, a false god is any concept which inhibits your power or incites your power to move negatively. The true power you have comes from the spirit, and its movement is known as emotion. The very word emotion comes from the Latin preposition e—from, and the verb *movere*, meaning to move. Thus the word means motion out from. Emotion is the only real motion you have. Physical motion is reflexive and follows the dictates of the inner motion (or emotion). When anger rises in the breast of an undisciplined man, he is compelled to express it in some fashion, either in the blow of the hand, the kick of the foot, or an explosive word from the mouth. What we know in everyday speech as a "slow burn" is simply the sinuous movement of an ugly emotion wrapping itself around and strangling all the vital and constructive movements. On the other hand, when love flowers in the human heart it makes a person good all over. It charms away his fears, dissolves his hates, relaxes his tensions and dictates every charitable and magnanimous word and act.

It is ideas which give rise to emotions. Every idea in the mind has its corresponding emotion. They are a wedded pair and inseparable. In the story of the Garden of Eden, woman is shown to come out of the side of man. Psychologically speaking, this means that emotion is born out of the structure of the idea or mental concept. This is a truth which anyone can observe for himself. Every one knows what happens when someone shouts "Fire!" in a crowded place. Similarly, we know what happens when mass emotion is handled by a disciplined person who talks and acts calmly and authoritatively in the midst of a crisis. On an individual level one can observe how an unexpected circumstance or a chance remark by another can depress or raise one's spirits. Words have been called triggers that set off the emotional forces. Not only words but any idea communicated to any of the senses is a trigger for emotional response of some kind. Something or someone presses buttons in the mind and the mind pulls levers to open valves for emotional force. A mother is told that her child's ailment is incurable and the pronouncement becomes the overpowering idea in her mind calling upon all the sleeping fears in the chambers of the psyche to come out and go to work. Everything she does is affected by this idea. A man gets it into his head that he has a jinx and that the fates are against him. He hesitates and is fearful. His constructive impulses and efforts are inhibited. He cannot move against his fear.

Now such ideas, opinions, theories, which act upon us and which stimulate us to act may be called gods. "Your god," says William James, "is whatever gives you climax." Whatever moves you to action or inhibits your action is to you a god. Whatever you believe in to the point of being affected by it, is a god to you. There are many superstitions and imaginings of the human mind to which people give power; many concepts that arouse emotional response and establish mental conviction. The concept itself is not a power, but it arouses your own spiritual power. Actually, there is but one power within you, one true God and that is your own spirit. As Paul said, ". . . there be gods many, and lords many, but to us there is but one God, the Father, of whom are all things . . ." (I Corinthians 8:5) Not that you contain God; rather, God contains you. In the depths of your subjective self is your personal door into the Universal and the Most High.

When Madame Schumann-Heink was a young girl of fifteen she had an audition with the director of the Vienna Opera Company who told her that she had no voice and that she should go back to her sewing machine. Now here is a god in the person of the opera director attempting to impress the mind of an eager young girl. He is the great man, the man of authority and knowledge. But this young girl is Ernestine Schumann-Heink, not yet great in the eyes of men but already sovereign in her young soul. She was not impressed by the words of the great man, so her spiritual power did not respond. He did not move her. Had this been someone less than the great artist, the director's words would have fallen on a sensitive, impressionable mind and awakened an emotional acceptance, and the girl would have returned to her housekeeping and grown up an ordinary hausfrau. In that case the opera director would have been a god she had believed in and his opinion would have been responsible for her meager existence. Actually, the girl's own spiritual power would have been the only true lord or creator of conditions. But she would have been limiting her own native power by emotional acceptance of the opera director's verdict. Madame Schumann-Heink's native spiritual power, however, created for her a life of great artistry and glory because she responded to her own positive feeling rather than to the negative opinion of the opera director.

Truly there is one power, one true God or creative cause living in and through every man. Many false gods people believe in are products of their ignorance of their own true natures. The Second Commandment bids you come to the understanding of the singleness of the spiritual power, to the awareness of its complete sovereignty and supremacy in all of your life.

It is the basic concept of the mind which produces its emotional life. That is why the Bible is so emphatic on the need for establishing the concept of one power. All who are born into the world embrace the limiting beliefs of ignorance. All will have to work through these beliefs and be born again into the realization of the power of God within them. All real growth and all real progress are toward self-realization and self-revelation. That which is involved in man is God and that which shall be evolved and discovered in man is the same. Man is God asleep and God is man awake. There is but one. This is at first a difficult concept for the mind which believes that only what it experiences through the senses is real.

The modern mind loves to praise itself for its freedom from superstition and witchcraft. Modern writers will often refer to the people in Biblical times as believers in demons and spirits, implying that moderns no longer believe in these creatures of fear's imagining. Modern religion makes claims to being monotheistic, that is, it upholds belief in one God. But to believe in one God doesn't always mean acting as if there were only one God. It frequently seems that we have simply changed the actors and the stage settings. The old play is just the same as it was and all manner of the mind's fears are still abroad to plague us. Every individual who has not experienced the creative Lord within himself will by the necessity of his psychology believe that creative power to be outside of himself. He will find it in other men, in animals and in sticks and stones of the inanimate world. He will deny his own power and affirm it as resident in everything but himself. More than this, he will go beyond the realm of the senses and populate the invisible ethers with gods who have power over him.

The common theory of disease is that it is an independent entity, existing somewhere apart from man and independent of him. Therefore he can "catch" a cold or be smitten by a germ or a virus which has in itself the capacity to modify the state of man's health even to the point of laying him low. Whatever we acknowledge to have power over us becomes to us a god and we may devoutly affirm that we worship one true God, but the facts of our living deny the affirmation of our lips. This is not to deny physical causes, nor to deny that physical causes bring about other physical conditions. It is to see that all physical causes are secondary causes, that there is only one primary cause and that is the mind and consciousness of man himself. The microbe of death is to be found in the blood-stream of the dying body, but it was the consciousness of death that created the microbe. Today the virus is one of the biggest and most powerful of gods in the pantheon of man. Many people who find it difficult and unreasonable to believe in an invisible spiritual power will without hesitancy accept the conclusion that a filterable (unseen) virus is the cause of their misery.

People need answers for their inquiries. They must know why they feel pain, why they have misery and unhappiness. Our ignorance of the one true power naturally assigns a cause to anything close at hand which offers a handy explanation. As an angry or cornered animal will attack anything which comes within its range, so will a sick mind, a mind in misery, tend to vent itself upon things around it. Self-knowledge is on the other side of these illusions.

About a hundred years ago the connection between emotions and health first began to be considered scientifically valid. Today most people know that emotions have something to do with their ulcers, their colds, their pains in the neck, as well as more serious ailments. But people still do not understand how their emotions originate. They do not realize that emotion is born of belief and that feeling flows from the central thought of the mind. What you believe and worship (and worship means to count worthy of attention) will awaken and come alive in you as an emotion. If you believe that there are malefic entities in the air or water outside of you which have power of fastening themselves upon you without your consent, then this belief to you is a source of anxiety and fear whether you know it or not. This belief is a button which, pressed under the right circumstances, will open the lid of the subconscious where abide all of the emotions, good and bad, and out will come first of all a mild anxiety, then like circus elephants in line and hooked trunk to tail, will come the more violent emotions of fear, foreboding and presentiment.

The traditional Christian doctrine of original sin is the doctrinal representation of the metaphysical and psychological truth that every one of us is born into limitation in this life, limitation that comes from unknowing. When the mind awakens to the spiritual truth of its own sovereignty, it puts away its sin because it is born again into an entirely new world. But it is first an entirely new world of mind and understanding and then a new world of experience. The person lives in this same old world of form and fact, but sees it and handles it differently in his thought, therefore experiences it differently in his circumstances. "In the world ye shall have tribulation, but be of good cheer, I have overcome the world."

The "world" is a New Testament term for the sleeping mind, for the mind that is unawakened to its spiritual capacities. This is the mind that deals with false beliefs, with fears and hates and bickerings, disease and misery and calamity. Every man must learn to overcome this mind or world within himself.

It is a psychological fact that the world we see is the world we are. Our psychology is forever being projected into our circumstances. To change one's psychology is to change one's world. There is one sure way of changing one's psychology and that is by diligent, constant, scientific prayer. Every kind of prayer is good, but scientific prayer reaches the goal more surely. By scientific prayer we mean a kind of spiritual reasoning or a meditation in which spiritual reasoning is dominant. By spiritual reasoning we mean a conscious, definite comparison of the beliefs of the outer world and the truths that are taught in the Ten Commandments to the end that one shall be forsaken, and the other will be accepted and enthroned as the mind's conviction.

No mind can change its belief without a good sound reason for doing so. A new theory must be reasonable to your mind before your mind will accept it as a conviction. In practical metaphysics we do not deal with doctrinal terms or religious beliefs. We are dealing with truths and principles which must first of all be demonstrable in reason. Some time in your life it will become reasonable to you to embrace the Second Commandment in all of its fullness. "Thou shalt have no other gods before me." Then you will put away your false beliefs. You will trust the purely spiritual power which you contact through your thought and you will not look with either fear or hope to anything outside of yourself, knowing that all things come through consciousness, through spiritual reality awakened in the consciousness of man. It will no longer seem reasonable or rational to you to believe that either promotion or defeat, sickness or health, can come from any source but this. This approach will lead you to a freedom the like of which you had not known and cannot know in any other way, and you will also know that heaven and hell are not outside the self nor beyond the grave. In a spiritual universe there is no such thing as time or space. Where there is no time, all things are present here and now. Heaven

will be seen to be only "the fulfillment of the soul's desire
and hell the misery of a soul on fire." (The Kasidah)

Once you realize that the spiritual power is without
shape or form, or the likeness of anything that we know on
earth, or which we can imagine in the mind, you will
make no more images of God. You will recognize that the
true God is purely spiritual, that it is without form or face
or figure, without any descriptive characteristics whatsoever. Therefore, the Second Commandment bids you not
to make any graven image. A graven image means two
things: It means something carved or fashioned by the
hand out of wood or stone or metal, or any material substance. It can also mean a picture or concept created in
consciousness by the mind's imagination. But when you
understand the nature of God, you will see the futility of
attempting to describe the Infinite from a limited, finite
point of view. "It is as high as heaven; what canst thou
do? deeper than hell; what canst thou know?" (Job 11:8)
The ancients declared that it was unlawful to represent
God by even so much as one jot or one tittle. A jot or a
tittle meaning the very smallest mark you can make with
a pencil. All forms and shapes, manifestations and representations, testify of God, but none of them in itself, or
all of them together, is adequate or big enough to describe
the Infinite Being. To represent God in anyway is to limit
His power to a particular mode of being. It is not only
unlawful and unscientific to represent God by some visual
image, but it is equally unlawful and unscientific for you
to represent God by any image of the mind. Any mental

picture of the Infinite imposes limitations on the very nature of God. Let, therefore, the Second Commandment be a constant guide to you in your thinking that you make no image of God out of physical things that are in the earth beneath, nor any image of God out of mental things that are in the heaven above.

The Commandment also says that thou shalt make no image or likeness of anything which is in the water under the earth. This refers to the subconscious realm in man which in the Bible is called the waters out of which all conscious life arises just as in the physical world, science tells us that all life upon the earth came out of the waters. To us the subconscious is a no man's land or a watery waste because it is mysterious and unknown. We tend to look upon it with awe or fear, and thus make a god out of it. Like all things else, it is a mode of the one Being, but it is not that one Being in his wholeness or his essence. Dreams come out of the unconscious and dreams are very impressive to us all. We sometimes erroneously assign to the imagery in a dream the power of God.

Dr. Quimby, in his famous experiments with his patients in mesmerism, often put his subject to sleep to have him diagnose disease in cooperation with a physician. His subject, Lucius, would prescribe some simple herb tea. The physician would give this prescription to his patient and the patient frequently got well. Now in many cases, the remedy which Lucius prescribed out of his sleep state was one which the physician himself had prescribed and had administered to his patient but which had not cured

the patient of his ailment. But after Lucius had prescribed it and the doctor had given it to the patient, the
patient recovered.

Much notable progress in mental science was made as a
result of these experiments. And, of course, one of the results was further proof that the healing power was of the
mind, that the herb tea had little or nothing to do with
the patient's getting well. In one case the physician had
prescribed the herb tea and it did no good. In the other
case the herb tea was also prescribed, but from a state of
trance, and it did some good. In one case the patient's
mind was unimpressed. In the other case it was impressed
and moved in awe by a man talking, his eyes closed, seem-
ingly communicating with another world. It was discovered that Lucius was reading the mind of the physician in
prescribing the herb tea and was not therefore bringing
any divine message from heaven but simply from himself
and the mind of another man.

To many people a person who would be unimpressive
with his eyes open becomes a god when his eyes are closed
and he talks out of his own subconscious. Do not make
the subconscious God. Do not take its dream image, its
conversation, for any more nor any less worth than you
would take the imagery and conversation of the conscious
world. The subconscious is important. Its imagery and
instructions are of vast importance, but like the conscious
mind, it is subject to both good and bad influences and
therefore cannot be considered a pure fountain or an in-
fallible source of wisdom. The oracle of ancient Greece

or the entranced mind of today may speak great and wonderful things, or it may speak lies. The only safe course in
this regard is the practice of that exercise which alone can
discipline both conscious and unconscious by the rule of
divine law, namely, prayer.

Out of the subconscious come our emotions. The conscious life is intellectual. The two together form our
consciousness. But because emotions arise out of this unseen and dark realm, because they are modes of the spirit's
function and action, people become magically impressed
by them and often make an emotion god. An ecstasy or
religious fervor is *a* god, but it is not *the* God. The mind
can be stirred by preaching or by incantation or by quiet
and steady conditioning, until the lid of Pandora's box is
opened and the emotions that have been locked in leap
out to work, directing and compelling the individual's expressions and actions. This, again, is not God. The emotions and movements are motions of the spirit, to be sure,
but they are not the whole or Holy Spirit. God is both
reason and emotion, both mind and spirit, and it is this
wholeness which we want to see standing behind all of the
modes of being.

A good way to understand it is to think of your own
mind. The mind functions through the five senses largely.
It sees and hears, tastes and smells, and feels. All of these
operations are evident. But the mind itself is never seen.
The mind thinks and originates ideas, reasons, and acti-
vates speech; manifests its powers in all of these ways, but

never shows itself. Nobody knows what mind is, though we see the results of its activity.

In the same way the great God, the infinite One, the single One, stands behind all his modes and functions so that we must never take any one manifestation as supreme and self-existent. A mind that can be stirred to great ecstasy by external sights and sounds can, by similar agents, be plunged into melancholy, fear and despair. The true God, when known in the mind, is sovereignty for that mind, in freedom and peace. The mind that is subject to its environment is a slave. It may surmise that the happy feeling which it finds stealing over it when it worships at some shrine, or when it goes into the woods and fields, is God. But this is an illusion. A man once said to me, "I can feel the presence of God much more on a Sunday morning when I go trout fishing in a mountain stream than when I sit in any church." I know exactly what he meant. Man's world is full of inharmony. Nature is harmony itself. In nature things are as they should be. All is in harmony with natural law. That is why man, when he leaves man's world and goes to the woods and streams— what Emerson called the sanative woods—feels a peace and harmony that are healing. This indeed is an aspect of God, but it is not the God of the First Commandment. God is not just a feeling. A person who can find peace only in the midst of nature, can find only misery in the midst of men. The mind that cannot originate its own peace, but is dependent upon its influences to find peace, will also be subject to the negative influences of life which will destroy its peace. Finding peace in nature is no better in the long run than finding peace in the cathedral. For you cannot carry nature with you any more than you can carry the cathedral with you into your office or your shop. The true God goes with you wherever you go and never leaves you nor forsakes you.

> If I ascend up into heaven, thou art there: if I make my bed in hell, behold, thou art there. If I take the wings of the morning, and dwell in the uttermost parts of the sea; even there shall thy hand lead me. (Psalm 139:8-10)

The true God is a wisdom resident in the mind which quickens the spirit, calls forth the proper emotion or mood to fit the time and circumstance. This wisdom recognizes only one power, purely spiritual, occupying no locality, therefore present everywhere, creator and sustainer of all forms, shapes, movements, processes and manifestations. This wisdom assigns no power to matter. Matter has no self-conscious intelligence, no volition, no capacity to change itself or to move any other piece of matter. No more can images in the mind or in the subconscious mind have power. Therefore, when any human mind sets up a concept, a theory or an opinion about causation being outside of itself, it is guilty of worshiping a false god.

The Commandment says that harm will result because God is a jealous God. Here the Commandment speaks of a higher truth in the terms of a lesser truth so that all may understand.

To be jealous means to be intolerant of another and to insist upon exclusive devotion. Intolerance of another is a peculiar law of the subjective mind in man. The subjective or deep self is responsive to the conscious mind's thinking. The subjective is the seat of the emotions so that the nature of its response is emotional. It will not respond, however, when there is division, indecision or argument in the conscious mind. If you are indecisive as to which of two propositions you should embrace, you will get no support from the deep self until you make up your mind. Of course you can ask for guidance on the matter and the deep self will provide it. Then you must make the decision in your conscious mind. After that the deep self will get behind your decision and be an invaluable working partner in your enterprises.

Again, let us suppose that you affirm that your wealth is from God but at the same time you are resenting the fact that your employer does not pay you enough. Your resentment suggests that you do not believe in the law of God as much as you think you do. Part of your faith is in humans and their institutions. Part of you is looking to the company or employer for increase. This is a divided faith and the subjective knows it and responds halfway. God is jealous. Of course you must understand that your wealth comes through people but not from them. When you attribute the power of causation to anything save the *I am*, you are setting up a rival to God and this spells trouble.

The Commandment speaks thus of jealousy in order to demonstrate to the mind which has set up false gods the principle of rivalry and opposition on its own level of understanding. If you pray to God for health and happiness, or for any good, and at the same time believe that certain people or certain shortcomings in you are preventing health and happiness, you are setting up in your mind, and therefore in your experience, an opposition. Then the mind's attention is divided between two opposing concepts. The mind loses its force for any constructive work, and the great power of God is unable to work fully through that mind.

Another way of saying this is that such a mind cannot concentrate. The very word concentration means mental movement in a circle around a central point. The practical application of this truth was nowhere better stated nor demonstrated than in the life and works of a friend of mine, a famous businessman and leader of men in many walks of life. He stated it early in his career to a group of men in his employ. "If you concentrate you will be accurate: if you are accurate you will be efficient: if you are efficient you will be successful." Surely this is the fundamental law of success. Certainly it was paramount in the remarkable career of the late General William Ottmann, former Commander of the New York Guard, and the late Chairman of the Board of the United States Printing and Lithographing Corporation whose words these are. He came to the discovery of this truth in his own practical experience with life. It is interesting and reassuring to notice that when any man finds an essential truth, it is not different from the essential truth which any other man found though they may have lived and worked centuries apart. The truth of the Bible is not for a bygone age. It is as alive and as practical for us today as it was when it was written. The law of life when discovered, experienced and practiced by any individual is not found to be different from the discovery of any other man. There is not a law for the businessman, another one for the farmer and another one for the engineer, artist or religionist. There is one law, or as the Bible says, one Lord. Actually, all the Bible has to say is this one thing: "Hear, O Israel, the Lord our God is one Lord (Law)." Success in any field or in any operation or enterprise depends upon efficiency then, and efficiency simply means the expenditure of energy with the least amount of waste.

With engineers who design our automobile engines, the biggest devil or oppositional factor is friction. They are continuously at work trying to overcome this with better alloys of metals, better lubricants and better design in general. An aeronautical engineer has to consider air resistance as his devil. A salesman must face what he calls the sales resistance of the public. There is no field of human thought or operation where this devil, or oppositional factor, is not found. Weak minds bow down before it and acknowledge it as God, and say there is no strength in us, no power, no means by which we can overcome this opposition. Strong minds know intuitively and out of practical experience that there is always a way out and over, and they work to prove it. "Unto you who fear my name shall

the Son of righteousness arise with healing in his wings."
(Malachi)

Practical metaphysics and divine psychology define the
supreme way of overcoming the oppositional factor. It is
applicable to every problem, and practicable in every field.
Go back to the source of the mind's consciousness, to the
wisdom of that infinite One of which it, the individual
mind, is a part. Understand that this purely spiritual
power which the individual mind in its thinking and its
feeling induces out of invisibility into visibility, is the only
true creative power. It is the substance and the existence
of all things. How much it will do for any individual is
utterly dependent upon his concepts and his own consciousness of it.

Your problems and sufferings are due to a limitation in
your own awareness of the one power. The negative is not
something actual, but is a denial of that which is actual.
Everything in life, including our thoughts, comes in pairs,
the eternal opposites, as they are called: spirit and matter,
negative and positive, sweet and sour, pleasure and pain,
hope and fear. There is no point in saying that one is real
and the other is not. They are both real in personal experience. Nothing is more real than pain to the one who
feels it. In any operation of the human mind within itself,
or upon matter outside of itself, these opposites have to be
reckoned with. First there is war, or a joining of the issue.
Then must come the death of one of the pair. In every
step forward the mind must overcome its thought of opposition and move forward with its ideal or dream. Only

the constructive ideal must be allowed to survive in the
human reason. In other words, the mind must be lifted up
beyond the opposition until it can see the fulfillment of its
goal irrespective of the opposition. Your fear that negates
your ideal must die; your ideal must live.

The Second Commandment speaks of this opposition of
forces in terms of personality, in which category it is
known as jealousy. In human affairs, jealousy means the
resentment of a rival for the affections of the one he loves.
The marriage contract enjoins us to select one spouse from
among all the world and, cleaving unto him or her alone,
forsake all others. In our society for over a thousand years
this arrangement has been found to be the most practical
one. In that society which is our mind, with its thoughts
and thought processes, the same principle holds true. In
fact the worldly rule is simply an adaptation or reflection
of the law as it is in heaven. The divine law of things demands one's exclusive devotion. It insists upon being first
in our reasoning and thinking. It is foundational, fundamental and primary, and your mind must establish itself
in this conviction and not waver and wonder if there is
any other cause or creative power.

Many times it will seem to your mind that there is a
force other than the purely spiritual one. For example, it
will seem plausible to you that your food or nutrition is
the sole foundation of your health. You will find much
evidence to confirm this view and your mind will tend to
wander away from its devotion to the spiritual principle.
You will begin to exalt and to love an external process or

substance. In placing your reliance upon the external food you forget and neglect the bread that comes from heaven which alone sustains and creates life. Because of this neglect of life, life is withheld from you. In human affairs you must have eyes only for the beloved and not see another. In the metaphysical realm the same is true. You must not "see" another power. Your fundamental faith must reside in the one purely spiritual power which moves through your thought and feeling, and in no other. The value of this lies in the fact that then no physical condition, nor external situation, nor other person can oppose, obstruct or restrain you in any way. Therefore there is nothing to fear, nothing to be anxious about, nothing to resist. There is only the Infinite One drawing nigh unto you because you have drawn nigh unto Him. Since He draws nigh unto you He fills you with His wisdom and His power and among men you become more than just your human self. If you neglect this rule, the amount of infinite wisdom and power active in your life becomes less and less as you allow less and less of it to enter. Thus your outer life dwindles and grows weak. In seeking an explanation for this weakness you will scout around in the external world for a cause and give your devotion to it. The Infinite One will seem to withhold His love and His favors from you, and you will want that which is withheld. But actually God keeps back none of His good from anyone. We are told, "Draw nigh unto God, and He will draw nigh unto you." (James 4:8)

The initiative is always with the individual so far as his

individual life is concerned. God has made the world and
established us in it. He has placed himself within us as an
oak tree is within an acorn. God has unfolded the cosmic
drama. Now the stage of action is transferred to the individual. There is only one Being. Hence there is only
one Actor. So the creative power in man, or at its point
of individualization, is still the one Infinite Being. When
man thinks and acts from his understanding, he is the
Infinite Being in action. As St. Theresa says:

> God has no other eyes to see his world than yours:
> no other hands to use it than yours: and no other
> feet to move across his world than yours.

Each of us is the instrument and the expression of the
power he understands and worships. The more clearly one
understands the nature of the Infinite Being, the more
perfectly he expresses God upon earth. When we understand this power, we do not divide up the world into good
and evil, good and bad powers. We find that all is unity.
We do not say, for example, that one should not bother
about what food he eats if he trusts in God. Every depart-
ment of knowledge and function is important. What we
are saying here is that one's dependence and one's faith
should be upon a purely spiritual power as the foundation
of all action and function on the part of the individual.
If a man has trust in food alone to bring him health, then
he is due to be disappointed, because he is guilty of giving
to a part of creation the power which belongs to the Creator alone. Food is a cause, but it is not a primary cause.

It is important, but it is not pre-eminently important. What is important is that man should worship the Ever-living One in all things. Good soil grows good food and good soil is alive with myriad forms of biological life. When we destroy the land through neglect of this principle, we are failing to observe the First and the Second Commandments in this regard.

In considering how God is a jealous God, we must lift our eyes above purely personal relationships between people and notice the relationship between ideas in the mind. For in failing to predicate your health and happiness upon the one creative power which is realized by your mind, you are depriving yourself of its attention and its love. Since you do not really love it, it will not love you. And it is not a question of personal pride, for God is not a human and what the Commandment calls his jealousy, is not jealousy as we recognize it in human affairs. The divine person is completely unlike any person that we know. God is law that never changes. He is an immutable law. The law is: what you give attention to—you will get results from; what you meditate upon—you will receive information about; what you give your heart to—will give itself to you. Be very careful what you are looking for, because you will find it. Be careful what you fall in love with, for it will surely come to live with you. If you fall in love with the sticks and stones of this world, then God is a jealous God withholding his love from you because he wants all of your heart.

The last of the Second Commandment sounds still more

human and personally vindictive when it speaks of visiting the sins of the fathers upon the children. But you
must remember that the Bible, including the Ten Commandments, is written for all levels of understanding.
Those who are at the bottom of the ladder of knowledge
understand things and processes only at the personal level.
This should not disturb you who can see the principle or
law at work at the personal level and can also follow it in
its higher workings as well. Whenever we look away from
the true power and place confidence in an object of creation rather than in the Creator, this is known as sin. More
particularly, when you allow your mind to move with your
fear rather than with your ideal, this is sin.

We understand our word sin to come from the ancient
Greeks in their practice of archery. When a man shot an
arrow and missed the bull's eye, he exclaimed, "I sinned."
When you are not doing or being what you want to do and
be, you are in a state of sin, psychologically and metaphysically speaking, because you are missing the mark of
your mind and soul. Your desire, your hope, your faith,
your prayer, your ideal, this is your mark. It is the mark
that God has given you to reach for, to pray for, to claim,
to realize through your confidence in the spiritual power.
But if instead of accepting your ideal, you allow your
mind to acknowledge obstacles in the way, you acknowledge restraints upon your power and you tend to accept
defeat; then you are in a state of sin. You are not believing
God and you are not believing in the reality of your hope
and prayer. Your power should move forth freely into ex-

pression. When it is dammed up by false beliefs in the mind, this is sin. And sin is the suffering of a soul on fire with its own misery. This is the hell the scriptures speak about which millions of people project outside of themselves into a state after death. Since the false beliefs which keep people in misery and in sin are rampant throughout the world, every child that is born into the world inherits to some extent these false beliefs and the fears and anxieties and negative moods that are associated with them. More particularly, a child born into a family where false beliefs and negative moods are dominant, inherits these as his patterns and in this way the sins of the fathers are visited upon the children.

A childish reading of this commandment will infer that God is a great big despot with a personality like some humans we know, and that he becomes angry with his children and vindictively visits the sins of the fathers upon the children as a punishment. But this is not so in precisely that way. The visiting of the sins upon the children is simply the working of the law. We are born without reason, so that all of our plastic nature is like an open book for the world to write upon. We accept the limitations of our parents and our teachers and those around us without knowing or realizing that in many cases we have hugged a viper to our breast or we have eaten the poisoned apple from the witch's hand. Our spiritual capacities have gone to sleep until such time as the kiss of the prince shall waken us to our true life again. Thus human life becomes a death in life and man is asleep to his spiritual powers and awake to the terrors and torments of the material world. He reasons about the everyday practical affairs of his life, and since knowledge of the single power is not within his consciousness, the main element of truth is outside of his reason. So his reasoning processes can never bring him to a real solution of his difficulties. But when this element of truth is awakened in the consciousness of man and he sees the supremacy of one spiritual power and the dependency of every physical thing and process upon this single power, and he understands that the terrors and diseases and failures he feared have no self-existence, that they are sustained by his own mind, then spiritual reasoning is born in the mind. The mind takes command of its own thoughts and emotions, cleanses its own temple and begins to rule its own world.

The coming of this awareness to the human mind is what is meant by the third and the fourth generation of "them that hate me," that is, of them who disavow and neglect me. The number three in the Bible always signifies completion of a process or piece of work; the number four signifies the completed form, expression and manifestation. They are used together here simply to indicate that somewhere between the three and the four a program will be completed. Those who hate me are those minds which turn away in ignorance of the one power. Since they deny it, it denies them. "I love them that love me." (Proverbs) Those who love me are those who come to an awareness of this power and think it not unreasonable to predicate their health and happiness and all things dear upon their remembrance of this power and their rejection of any other. So that no matter what your inheritance of sin or limitation may have been, the moment you come to the awareness of God's presence in your mind and heart, you are free of the past, the patterns are broken. "Your sins which were as scarlet shall be as white as snow" (Isaiah) and your whole progress from this point forward is from death to life.

Assume its Nature

**THOU SHALT NOT TAKE THE NAME OF
THE LORD THY GOD IN VAIN; FOR THE
LORD WILL NOT HOLD HIM GUILTLESS
THAT TAKETH HIS NAME IN VAIN.**

WHAT DOES IT MEAN to take the Lord's name in vain?
Does it mean to swear? What does swearing mean? Does
it mean to use profane language or does swearing mean to
take an oath as in a courtroom where a witness swears to
tell the truth, the whole truth and nothing but the truth?
It means all these things but much more besides. Whatever is debased has fallen down from its base and is weak,
invalid, unavailing, unsubstantial and therefore vain.

Profane language makes a great show of strength. The
person who sprinkles his language with vulgarisms sounds
assured and forceful at first hearing. He wields a psychological advantage over sensitive minds and that is precisely
why such a person resorts to profanity. He conceals his
weakness by browbeating others. It is a bad habit and like
all bad habits it takes its toll somewhere along the line.

The persistent swearer is confessing his inadequacy and lack of mental discipline. The violence of his emotion is self-destroying; thus he is, metaphysically speaking, constantly giving his subconscious suggestions of inferiority and mediocrity.

On the other hand, every realistic thinker knows the value of salty speech in the right place at the right time and the importance of slang phrases and even vulgarisms strategically used. The Bible is above all things practical and it is not inveighing against the bad taste of coarse language alone. It is also discussing what is a far weightier matter. Namely, that vocal expressions alone carry no power in themselves. Words in themselves are only symbols. A person may use violent language but unless the source of his strength is in spiritual understanding, his violent language is only a show and a facade, a vain and powerless thing.

There are two kinds of language, basically. There is the language of vocal sounds and there is the spiritual language of moods and motives, deep inside a person. The language of the spirit is a silent tongue, a still small voice. It is in all nature, in men and animals and to some extent in plants. As little as we sometimes realize it, there is nevertheless a communication between all things upon the spiritual level. As Kipling points out in his famous poem:

"Oh, East is East, and West is West, and
    never the twain shall meet,
Till Earth and Sky stand presently at
    God's great Judgment Seat.

> But there is neither East nor West, Border,
>   nor Breed, nor Birth,
> When two strong men stand face to face,
>   though they come from the ends of the earth!"

They come from the opposite ends of the earth and speak entirely different languages and are unable to understand each other's vocal sound. But they are two strong men, two men of character, disciplined and developed, and therefore they can understand and get along with each other. Character will recognize character, strength will honor strength and become the basis for understanding. An infant who cannot speak knows when someone loves it; growing things respond to a "green thumb"; a dog understands his master and the master understands the dog. This universal awareness of being is basic, it is God, it is the *I am* of the Scriptures.

When this basic state of being becomes aware of a particular situation, this realization is called its word. Word is the definition of the undefined. It is the specialization or particularization of the universal. What you as an individual are conscious of as your thought-feeling is your word, though it never be vocalized or clothed in speech. To think and feel is to speak in the basic language of the spirit. Two people who are, as we say, "close" can speak to one another without using words or other outward signs of communication. In short, in the spirit's language, thoughts are words. It is these words which are creative. When John says that "in the beginning was the word," he refers to the spiritual word, not a vocal sound. They may sometimes coincide—the inner word of the spirit and the outward expression—but not necessarily. When they do, power is released and results in action. The spiritual word is in and by itself creative; when the inner and the outer words combine, they are together creative. But the outer word without the inner word is vain as sounding brass or tinkling cymbal.

To "take the name of the Lord" does not mean to write or sound the letters G O D. It does mean to speak in the spiritual language. It means to take the nature of life and livingness and direct it to some end or purpose or action. Name means "nature" and the nature of the divine being is life. Only God is life. All other things have life and are dependent upon the Ever-living One. To "take the name" of stone, or participate in the state of being of a stone, would be to silence consciousness, to be impervious to outside stimuli and unaware of any urge or impulse. To "take the name" of musician would be to express harmony in sound. To "take the name" of chemist would not be to have a letterhead printed saying chemist or to have the word chemist painted on an office door or to hang out a shingle saying chemist. These in themselves would mean nothing if you did not know the laws of the chemical elements. To take the name of chemist would mean to put into practice the knowledge of the chemical elements and their relationships. To take the name of anything means to act upon your knowledge and understanding of that which the name represents. God is life and the nature of that life is, as we have seen, consciousness or the awareness of being. To know and act upon this knowledge is to worship the self-existent God.

Whenever you think and feel, consciousness is in action for good or bad. Consciousness is the creative factor in life. Thinking makes consciousness, makes us aware, and consciousness makes experience. To think of limitation, is to take the Name in vain. When a person falls down in his mind before difficult conditions or situations, when he quavers and fears and accepts the sense evidence of defeat, he is taking the Name in vain for he is misusing the marvelous powers of being and awareness, and thus limiting his progress in life. For it is a vain and fruitless exercise to think negatively, to indulge in the death wish. It makes trouble and brings misery. It is to no good purpose that a man should dwell on anything in his mind but order and the positive force of living. Man is a result of what is in his mind, and mind is a measure of the infinite good. Mind is always measuring, defining, thinking and choosing what it shall experience.

This Third Commandment is another directive from infinite wisdom telling us to occupy the mind with the great truth of a single power in order that the mind will not wander among material things and measure itself by appearances only. Whenever our mind does this we have to bring it back to the central truth. Such disciplinary action will pay big dividends in health and happiness. Then the mind takes up the name or nature of divine being, not in vain, not uselessly and fruitlessly, but positively, constructively, bringing divine law and order, health and happiness, into the individual existence. A mind occupied with the central truth of God is centralized and still, poised and confident. The mind which leaves this center in its thinking runs frantically around the periphery, looking into this and concerning itself with that. It finds hundreds of things to worry about, thousands of things to be vexed with, until it becomes a centerless, wandering prodigal in a shadow world of its own creation. A neurotic is a mind which thinks confusedly about too many things. A God-centered mind can never become neurotic.

So in the divine science of the mind we always correct what we see and hear by what we know. If we see sickness we remember that divine being cannot be sick, that sickness is due to the mind's involvement in material strains and vexations. We know that what a sick mind believes is not true, and in our thought we deny it for him. This corrects our own thought so that we do not take the Name in vain, and it tends to help others as well. Every distorted picture in the world which comes to our attention comes there for correction. That consciousness which has the true standard of one power can correct the picture. All others must repeat the error.

A friend of mind translates the Third Commandment directly from the Hebrew in these words:

> Thou shalt not raise the name of the eternal, the creator of thy life, for destruction, for the eternal will not hold guiltless the one who will lift up his name for evil. (B. Law)

This translation emphasizes that to take the Name in vain means to destroy one's life. To turn the splendid powers of mind toward hate or anger, dishonesty, resentment, or self-pity or overweening ambition, is to direct the creative forces towards one's own destruction. The Eternal will not hold such a one guiltless for the reason that the Eternal is law, and law is action and reaction, mathematical, immutable, just and certain.

This Commandment, in its usual translation, like the others, is couched in language that suggests God as a great person holding a personal grudge against a human being for transgressing a heavenly statute. Of course this is only the surface meaning and appears only at that level of understanding which is still seeing life as a personality and form. We have seen that beingness is a divine fact, and it is divine life. It is the only life there is. Because of it all creatures have life. Man or mind is a creation which can think about this, measure it, adapt and modify it into various experiences. Life is and will always be. But for man to be or not to be is within the measure or decision of his mind. To think so as to establish a new state of consciousness, is what is meant by taking the Name.

Consciousness or *I am*, or what is known as our personal psychology, gives the law to our objective world. That is why it and it alone is the real oath. An oath is not a blue streak of profane words only, but an established state of consciousness which insures a definite result. To swear an oath means either to utter a profane statement with the mouth using the word God or some other religious word or expression, or to vow or to make a solemn promise with an appeal to some sacred or revered person, place or thing. When a man in his speech suggests that God damn another man, that is one kind of oath. But, as we have seen, it is a superficial thing so far as insuring any result is concerned.

The old story about the men who were discussing the relative powers of ecclesiastical and civil authorities is apropos. One said, "A judge can only say you be hanged, while a bishop can say you be damned." Whereupon the other replied, "Yes, but when a judge says you be hanged, you are hanged." In other words no man, however lofty or holy his position, can damn another man. Only God can damn, which is to say only the law of consciousness self-invoked can damn a person into failure or misery. God, the Universal Being, does not willfully damn anyone. The decision is always with the individual. "All judgment is given unto the Son." (Jesus) So no person by any awful-sounding oath of words has any authority whatsoever to affect any other person, providing the other person knows this truth. Even if the oath is sworn by or in the name of some revered or sacred object or person, that gives it no validity or power whatever, save the ignorant awe which it inspires in the mind of one who does not know the spiritual law.

A man's oath, if it comes from his heart, his spirit and not just from his mouth, is valid for himself. It is the heart that gives it validity. When a person goes into the courtroom, for example, lays his left hand upon the Bible, raises his right hand and swears to tell the truth, the whole

truth and nothing but the truth, we know that his oath
insures performance only insofar as it comes from his heart
or inner consciousness. For we know that a man may take
such an oath yet perjure himself. The holy Bible, as a
book, is not able to guarantee the performance of his word,
nor is the majesty of man's law court and robed judge.
The custom of swearing by the Bible, by heaven or the
Holy City or by "all that's good and holy," carries the
implication that the respected thing or place makes
the oath binding. In his teaching Jesus makes it clear that
the respected object does not make an oath binding.

> Again, ye have heard that it hath been said by them
> of old time, Thou shalt not forswear (perjure) thy-
> self, but shall perform unto the Lord thine oaths:
> but I say unto you, swear not at all; neither by
> heaven; for it is God's throne: nor by the earth; for
> it is his footstool: neither by Jerusalem; for it is the
> city of the great king. Neither shalt thou swear by
> thy head, because thou canst not make one hair white
> or black. But let your communication be Yea, yea;
> Nay, nay: for whatsoever is more than these cometh
> of evil. (Matthew 5:33-37)

Jesus' teaching is always directed to those who know the
divine law of consciousness and who live by it. To them
there is no need to swear by outer things or to make impressive statements to convince. A man's consciousness is
his law, and it is his word. His word is his bond. This
state is a holy covenant between a man's inner self and his
outer self, or between God and man. The heart's word is

a solemn contract which is never broken. It is a contract between the inside doer and the outside act. An unthinking person may swear or vow one thing and do quite another. A person's real vow lies in his consciousness. What he says may or may not agree with his consciousness, but what he does will most certainly be a mathematically exact reproduction of his thought and feeling. Some people cultivate the habit of deceit with their words so we have to watch their acts to see what kind of persons they are.

When a person's thought is clear upon this point he is free from a thousand superstitions, religious and otherwise. He can then perform unto the Lord his oath, that is, he will work with his own consciousness in meditation and prayer to establish convictions of good, knowing that these will confirm themselves in action. He will make no wild protestations against evil or evil doers. He will not feel it necessary to make a drama out of his promises and intentions. He will assume the right consciousness within and allow it to confirm itself by its own law and through its own power. He will hallow the Name and rest in the law and trust no promised good and fear no prophesied evil which is not in his own consciousness. Christians who have learned to invoke the name of Jesus in their prayers will realize the grave import of such an invocation.

Sabboth

REMEMBER THE SABBATH DAY, TO KEEP
IT HOLY. SIX DAYS SHALT THOU
LABOUR, AND DO ALL THY WORK: BUT
THE SEVENTH DAY IS THE SABBATH OF
THE LORD THY GOD: IN IT THOU SHALT
NOT DO ANY WORK, THOU, NOR THY
SON, NOR THY DAUGHTER, THY MAN-
SERVANT, NOR THY MAIDSERVANT,
NOR THY CATTLE, NOR THY STRANGER
THAT IS WITHIN THY GATES: FOR IN
SIX DAYS THE LORD MADE HEAVEN AND
EARTH, THE SEA, AND ALL THAT IN
THEM IS, AND RESTED THE SEVENTH
DAY: WHEREFORE THE LORD BLESSED
THE SABBATH DAY, AND HALLOWED IT.

LET YOUR MIND FIND REST and you rule the world.
This is the meaning of the Sabbath. Great power is char-
acterized by quietness of movement. Niagara thunders
and boils and its power is dissipated. But when the force
is channeled into a tube and over a wheel there is little

noise but great concentration and direction of power. The supreme power is God. The greatest power among men derives from the contemplation of God. Such contemplation brings the mind away from torment and into rest. This is not a deathlike rest, but a dynamic rest of consciously controlled power. Biology recognizes rest and motion as the two great laws of life, inherent in all living things.

The Fourth Commandment deals with motion and rest, and thus the Great Law codifies this truth along with the other nine. The law of the Sabbath is the law of rest for the mind, for the body and for both together. It is based upon the recognition that everywhere in nature this truth is fundamental: life is alternation between work and rest.

Rest is the great replenisher and the greatest rest is found in the state of mind called faith. The road to faith is work which is the labor of the mind. The only real work man has on this earth is to find the presence of God within himself. The way is laid out and marked clearly by a thousand thinkers of the past.

The Ten Commandments are the mileposts for the mental journey that takes one to the greatness of himself. Yet the average man takes every other road but this. He labors long and hard to understand the phenomena of life, to find the treasure which is forever hidden within. All external labor is reflexive and confirmatory. A person with many limiting beliefs or false gods may labor very hard in the external sphere of his life. He may struggle and strain and bend every effort for success, yet find him-

self an unproductive worker always seeking a prize which
eludes him. This is because the labor of his mind is unproductive. Every man's mind should lay hold on God,
the greatest good and the greatest treasure, the basis
and the substance of all things else.

The Fourth Commandment refers basically to this mental labor which accomplishes the great work. This commandment contemplates you as working in your own mind
to destroy the mind's illusions by spiritual reasoning, casting down its idols and turning out its false beliefs and
erroneous opinions. This work is illustrated elsewhere in
the Bible by the account of the Master going into the
temple and casting out the merchants and money-changers.
". . . It is written, My house shall be called a house of
prayer; but ye have made it a den of thieves." (Matthew
21:13) The mind is the house of God where consciousness,
the divinity, dwells. Of course the body is also called the
temple of God but in the sense of an outer court to an
inner sanctuary. The mind is the first temple. A troubled
mind is occupied by thieves and usurpers, for a fear is a
thief stealing the strength and purpose of the mind. Any
opinion which exalts created things above the creative
cause is a usurper of mental space and a despoiler of the
soul's peace. These must be cast out by the master of life.
To become such a master is your task and labor. More
particularly, every time you are faced with a problem you
will find it necessary to cast out the false occupants of the
mind and to give place to the consciousness of God as the
only power.

Another name for this kind of labor is prayer. Prayer is a joining process by which you mentally unite yourself to the good you seek. This good is in consciousness; it is God. So prayer is joining up with God again. When this point of union is reached the mind rests and practices the Sabbath.

Thus the Great Law intends something far more significant and fundamental than the ordinary practice of refraining from physical work on Sunday or whatever other day is celebrated as the Sabbath. Every day of the week has been used at some time by some group or sect as the Sabbath day. The day of the week is relatively unimportant. What is important is that you observe one day out of seven as a day of rest and replenishment.

The proportion of one day in seven seems to be a fundamental law of nature. There have been attempts in the past history of man to change this proportion, as for example, the one day in ten scheme of the French Revolution. Experience has shown that the proportion of six days of labor and one day of rest is right for man.

There are remarkable instances of the authority of the number seven in other parts of nature, the table of periodicity in the chemical elements, for example, and the seven colors of the spectrum.

The word *Sabbath* means seven, that is, the seventh day, or the seventh month, or the seventh year, or the seventh measure of whatever order you are dealing with. The word *Sabbath* also means restoration, restitution, atonement, wholeness, repose and rest. To suppose that this

refers only to the rest taken on one day of the week from
the labor of the other six days, is far too literal an interpretation of the meaning of the Sabbath. If we were to read
all of the Ten Commandments in this literal fashion, then
it would be easy to find salvation. To realize all the bene-
fits such as health and long life and prosperity that are
promised as the result of keeping the Commandments of
God, all we should have to do would be to announce with
our lips that we believed in one God and no other; never
to use the word God in any vulgar or profane sentence; to
refrain absolutely from all labor on the Sabbath, such as
washing the car or cooking the dinner, for literalists say,
in this observance, that you must not even make a fire to
cook the dinner on the Sabbath day. Ancient teachers used
to say that if a beggar came to your house and you reached
your hand outside of the window to give him some alms,
that was work and was a profaning of the Sabbath day.
But if the mendicant thrust his hand through the window
and inside the house, then it was all right to drop some
alms into his hand, for that would not be labor.

The easy assumption that the literal meaning is all there
is to the Ten Commandments and that salvation can be
found by such a literal observance, was given its answer by
Jesus. When the rich young ruler asked him what he
should do to attain eternal life, Jesus told him to keep
the Commandments. "All these," the rich young man said,
"I have kept from my youth up. What lack I yet?" Whereupon the Master told him to sell all that he had and give
it to the poor and come and follow him. The account

closes by saying that the rich young man turned sorrow-ingly away because he had great possessions. We must assume that the young man had kept all the Command-ments in a literal way and had not found the conviction of everlasting security. Because if he had kept the real Commandments, which are not commandments at all but principles of thought and action, he would not then have been in the position in which Jesus found him, the posi-tion of having too many possessions. For certainly wealth in terms of money and property is not a crime, nor is it in itself a deterrent to spiritual progress. What hinders or impedes a man is always the thinking in his mind. The real possessions are in consciousness.

No man owns any tangible property. It is loaned to him only. It is what he thinks about it and what he does with it that determines his happiness. The young man had too many possessions in the mind. His materialism was not in the ownership of physical wealth but in the fallacy of putting trust and reliance in material things. A man may be wealthy in this world's goods and still keep his trust rightly placed in the true God and thus win eternal se-curity. On the other hand, a man who is poor in this world's goods, and yet puts his hope in these things, is a far worse materialist than the wealthy man. His philoso-phy also denies the true God. With every thought directed toward acquiring physical things, he takes himself further and further away from the true security which is rest of mind in a spiritual principle. So one may keep all of the Commandments in a literal fashion and still come short of

the glory of God in his daily life. Many a person remem-
bers how, as a child, he was made to conform to the strict
discipline of the Sabbath observance because his parents
and teachers felt that this was the proper and meaningful
way to observe the seventh day. Many people today still
keep the Sabbath in this way. They rest their bodies from
the weekday job, but fail to rest from their nervous tension
or their worry, and worry is labor and labor is a profana-
tion of the Sabbath of God.

Remember the Sabbath day to keep it holy. Holiness,
like all else, begins in the mind and if one carries around
a problem in his mind he is certainly not remembering the
Sabbath nor observing it. The words *holy* and *wholly*
have a common root: whole. A mind with a problem is
not whole. Such a mind is split between two ideas. Its
devotion is divided. Its fear wars with its hope. Wholeness means all of one kind, undivided, entire, complete.
The worried mind is none of these. This is not to say that
all worry is wrong. The mind must work to accomplish.
It is prolonged worry or the same pattern of worry repeated over and over again that is unwise. Every mind
should learn to work through its worry and come to a
point of rest in the truth of God. This is the teaching of
the Fourth Commandment. No difficulty should be prolonged beyond its time. No troublesome situation need
be endured forever. No tension should be suffered as a
continual burden. These things can all be solved by the
application of the law of mind. When they are solved

through mental realization the mind returns to peace and that peace is what is meant by the Sabbath.

Our minds move from rest to rest or from faith to faith. In between these two points we labor with worry, concern, tension, desire, hope and fear. In fact, whenever a new desire or hope or wish comes to the mind, the mind's peace is taken. It is restless until it does something with its desire or new idea. Every wish or desire brings with it its necessary opposite principle, its negative opposition. The farmer wants to go south, but who will milk his cows during the winter? A businessman wants to replace his plant equipment, but high taxes seem not to allow him. A man wants a certain job, but in order to get it he must be a member of the union and the union is already full. A sensitive and capable person wants to work and create, but sickness plagues him. A job holder drifts from job to job because of personality difficulties; he cannot get along with other people.

Every human problem has its two parts, the positive desire that rises from within in response to conditions and the negative factor which arises in the mind when it looks at its circumstances. The false gods are always after us, calling upon us to bow down and worship them. We hear the voice of the true God within urging us to dream and dare and do. "Speak unto the children of Israel, that they go forward." (Exodus 14:15) But we hear a hundred voices outside the mind urging caution, hesitation and compromise and even acceptance of defeat. "Faith cometh by hearing," says Paul, and that voice to which you give your ear will condition you and establish its law within you.

Faith is a position of confidence, assurance and rest in the mind which comes from listening to the true voice of God within. Faith, too, has its opposite number and it is called fear. Fear is simply faith turned inside out, because fear is faith in the wrong thing. Fear is a conditioning of the mind. Fear is the mind's acceptance of the negative side of any problem. Fear is a conditioned state of the mind which is established when the mind gives too much attention to the false voices of the false gods.

Of course, someone will say, "Well, you cannot ignore circumstances." Indeed, you cannot. But you can think about them in a positive way. Someone will say, too, "The facts do not lie." And that is true, too. But the person who interprets the facts may lie unknowingly. The truth is that no fact is final. Every fact is subject to the law of change. The whole world of circumstances and conditions is subject to the law of change. Look out your window at any building or structure or at the body of any man, animal or bird and there is one judgment that flows from your mind with Jovian authority and that is: This, too, will pass. Every created thing is subject to change and will pass away. We mothproof our garments, develop antirusts for metals and antirots for woods, but everywhere we look all things, like Proteus, are constantly assuming different shapes in spite of all we can do.

Now particularize this law and apply it to yourself. That pain in your body will pass away if you will let it.

That old fear or resentment will pass away if you will let go of it. The farmer can find a way to go south and the businessman can find a way to stay in business. That way will be shown when the mind's fascination with the negative aspects of the particular problem is broken. Two men, in passing through a thick jungle, became separated from one another. One called and shouted for his friend but could get no response. He finally came upon him in an open clearing, standing stock-still and frozen like a statue. Upon coming closer he found that his friend's eyes were fixed upon a large snake in a tree. The snake was fascinating him. Had the scene been allowed to unfold, the snake would have crushed his victim without pain, for the man was unconscious and without mind and will. The snake was scared away, the spell was broken and the frozen man returned to consciousness.

The same thing happens between you and the things that you fear. This world is full of the vivid descriptions of terrors and troubles and sufferings. Error is on the lips of nearly everyone, but truth can rarely find a home in human estimation. It is despised and rejected of men, and has no form or comeliness that we should desire it. (Isaiah 53:2-3) What the mind is fascinated by it will inevitably create. Man is made in the image and likeness of God. He repeats the pattern of his creator in his own operations by making his own particular world of experience out of his own image after his own likeness. If you become fascinated with the pathology of disease, you are in danger of making more disease at the same time that you are taking infinite pains to cure it. If you become convinced of an independent power of evil existing outside of you, you will be building a structure by day yet tearing it down by night. Mind works like a syllogism: what you accept as your premise you will inevitably find in your conclusion. See the world populated with terrors and evil things which can move against you, without your consent, and in everything that you do you will find what appears to be some jinx or some demon, some conspiracy of the fates to ruin your plans and prevent the fruitfulness of your efforts.

Mind must be brought back again and again to the one truth that there is only one power and it is operating through the imagery of one's own mind. This is the purpose of prayer and it is also the purpose of the Sabbath, for the Sabbath is but a form of prayer. The mind cannot stay too long in the world of the senses. They will pull it down into the limiting imagery of fear and error. Everywhere you go you will see truth and error in combat. You will see injustice, suffering, man's inhumanity to man, poverty and limitation of all sorts. You will sense the strains and stresses of people trying to solve their problems and to get along. Every man must have some way to "overcome the world" and rise above it. It is impossible for him to live always with its strains and stresses. For this reason the Great Law has set aside one day in seven for our spiritual reflection and commanded us to do no manner of work. It was for a similar purpose that we are directed when we pray to enter into our inner chamber and close the door, so that we would not be distracted by the sense perceptions of the world and so that we might think of the higher principle and commune with our Father in heaven and restore a more wholesome imagery to the mind.

Every true prayer is a scientific reordering of the mind by which the attention is withdrawn and abstracted from the diversity of the sense world and returned to the unity of the First Commandment. The mind must be brought back from its wanderings in matter and returned to the Father's house where there is peace and nourishment and strength for the next day's activity in the world. You will find that in every personal problem the mind has gone away from this center and is acknowledging other powers. Thus, to solve any personal problem you must bring the mind back from the world of the senses to the consideration of this central truth in order to restore the mind to its proper dignity and to a proper sense of its own authority in its world. Prayer is the denial of the despotism of conditions and the affirmation of the sovereignty of the spirit. There is no problem that will not yield to this kind of prayer. There is no situation that cannot be bettered by this practice.

But I would warn the reader that it is not a matter of simply going "within." Sometimes the "within" is a den of thieves or a chamber of horrors. Prayer is not going within the human personality, but it is going within to the principle of life. Instead of allowing the mind to be fascinated by the parade of limitation set up by the senses, take it to the consideration of the First Commandment.

Walk it around and around this great fundamental truth until the mind becomes fascinated and absorbed. The senses are all under your control, and with assurance and practice you can master them.

A simple illustration in everyone's experience will show how the senses can shut out all surrounding phenomena and become centered upon the consideration of a single thing. Every household has one member, usually the husband, who can become so absorbed in the newspaper, or book, that the wife or another member of the family may speak to him and he will not hear. He is absorbed, engrossed, in his reading matter. His sense of hearing has been abstracted from all things around him and he hears only what he gives attention to. In prayer practice we shall hear only our Father's voice which is the voice that gives us authority over the devils of this world and blesses us with peace of mind and fruitfulness of effort.

That the Sabbath is not just a religious rule but a fundamental of our nature may be seen in the fact that we spend one-third of our lives in sleep. Every night is a Sabbath which "knits up the ravelled sleeve of care" and retrieves the senses from the vexations of the day. It is popularly supposed that we sleep in order that we may rest. But what rests when we sleep? Certainly not the physical body. The heart continues to beat and never has a moment's rest (except the pause between systole and diastole) from the time of our birth until the time of our death. The lungs do not rest. The process of inspiration and expiration by means of which fresh air is supplied to the blood goes on by night and by day. The same is true of our stomach, our glands, our kidneys, and of all the other mysterious operations of the body. The nails and the hair continue to grow during sleep as during the waking hours. The skin is more active during sleep, for a person in good health while sleeping will expel from his body, by perspiration and without resorting to any artificial means of promoting it, twice as much matter as in the same period of time while awake. And nothing is excreted through the skin that has not been thoroughly used by the body it leaves. During sleep, the brain receives impressions showing that not only the optic, auditory, olfactory and gustatory nerves are more active during sleep, but that the corresponding cerebral nerve centers are active.

The subconscious mind or deep self or soul never sleeps. This is shown by the fact that it is always amenable to suggestion and is responsive to outside stimuli. Everyone has had ample experience to show that the mind does not sleep. The mind is a great traveler in dreams and a great actor. Mind is a great alarm clock. If you tell it before going to sleep that you wish to awaken at seven, it will generally awaken you precisely at that hour. Has something in you been awake all night watching the clock? And everyone has had the happy experience of going to bed struggling for the answer to a problem and awakening in the morning and having the subconscious mind present the solution to him full-blown. All the evidence goes to show that there is no such thing as absolute rest. "Nature has no pause," said Goethe, "and visits with a curse all in-action."

Then what is this thing called sleep and what purpose does it serve? Why are men, as well as the vegetable and animal kingdoms, required to spend on an average eight out of every twenty-four hours in sleep? If rest, as we know it, is not the answer, then why should we spend all of this time in a state of dormancy and inactivity? Some people, including the philosopher Kant, have thought that this was a great waste of time on nature's part and have endeavored to decrease the number of hours spent in sleep. They succeeded only up to a point. It seems quite safe to say that nobody ever will succeed in revising nature's statute which allots six days to labor and one to rest. Sleep is an inexorable master and an inevitable necessity.

> Every night of our lives sleep descends upon us like an armed man; prostrates us with barbarous indifference on beds of down or straw, and closes up all our communications with the workaday world, as in death. (John Bigelow)

Nobody can postpone sleep for very long. No matter how pressing your interests and pursuits, no matter how much you think that certain enterprises depend upon your thoughts and acts, finally there will come the time when you must give over the controls into another hand. You may postpone sleep seventy-two or ninety-six hours or possibly more, but finally the inexorable master will levy his tribute and you will be unconscious of everything you have done in the past and all you are planning to do in the future. It is necessary periodically for you to drop the burdens of the world and your conscious considerations of them. It is necessary that you let go of grudges, wounds, torments and vexations. These can only be assuaged by the gentle presence of sleep. The most tremendous healing force we know is sleep and every good physician knows that when his medicine or other treatment will not help, sleep will help. With all our science we have not yet mastered the common cold. The most frequently prescribed remedy for this troublesome malady is bed and rest.

Sleep is the great deliverer from the domination of the phenomenal world. All religion prescribes it, but nature insists upon it. When the cares and burdens of everyday life become too heavy for the human psyche to bear, sleep walks close beside us and conducts us away from it all and into another existence in which we abide for a time and from which we return regenerated.

The remarkable changes that follow upon a good night's sleep all suggest that we have walked with a Providence and been under the tutelage of a wisdom far superior to anything that we know of in our waking hours. "The morning hour," says a German proverb, "has gold in its mouth." If our sleep has been good we awaken refreshed and strengthened. The mind is calm and clear, conditions and animosities are soothed, we are relaxed from the tensions of the day before. Why is it that our mind is so much more alert in the morning? The problems which puzzled us the night before seem solved without a strug-

gle. Why should it be so easy in the morning to find that
lost article we searched for in vain in the evening? Why
did the school child have so much trouble in memorizing
the poem in the evening, only to discover that with the
morning the words came accurately and smoothly? The
answer to these questions is that in sleep we are taken over
by our better nature, by God, if you please.

Sleep is undoubtedly designed to promote the growth of
spiritual wisdom in us in contradistinction to the many
illusions of the sense-world. The considerable portion of
our lives which we spend in sleep is not less important
than those hours which we spend in wakefulness. Prayer
is a form of sleep because it abstracts the senses from the
burdens of this world and returns them to truth. Therefore the man of prayer is cooperating with the great
ordinance of nature which prescribes sleep at periodic intervals.

The man of prayer undoubtedly makes much progress
even during sleep. He will place great emphasis upon all
forms of sleep, not only that upon his bed, but prayer and
relaxation and all exercises which deflect the mind from
its burdens to that principle which can lift man above his
burdens. Something flows into us in these times of sleep
which we cannot get from any other source.

> The nobler part of the soul is thus united by ab-
> straction to higher natures and becomes a participant
> in the wisdom and foreknowledge of the gods. (John
> Bigelow)

The spiritual growth and therefore the real progress of our life, is not interrupted when we sleep. On the contrary, it is more than ordinarily active. Job says:

> In a dream, in a vision of the night, when deep sleep falleth upon men, in slumberings upon the bed, then he openeth the ears of men and sealeth their instruction, that he may withdraw man from his purpose and hide pride from man; he keepeth back his soul from the pit and his life from perishing by the sword. (Job 33:15-18)

Sleep is a divine ordinance which withdraws man from his human opinions and erroneous views of things. These cause him to quarrel with matter and with his fellows, to strain and to strive for things which God has already given him and which only await his acceptance. Sleep shows man a higher way. It humbles his pride, causes him to know that he is not indispensable to this earth or to any program he has initiated upon it.

When you get to thinking that your business cannot run without you, ask yourself how you would run it if you could not sleep and have the advantage of consultation with a superior partner, a senior partner and a superior wisdom every night. All things and processes upon the face of the earth are indeed given into the dominion of man, but he is but a little child and knows not how to come in or to go out. In all his operations his hand has to be guided by a larger hand and this guidance comes to him in sleep, in all of its forms, when the consciousness is withdrawn from the material world and made obedient to a higher knowl-

edge. This is an absolute necessity of our nature. Without
it we would burn ourselves out and fall into the pit which
Job mentions. We would pierce ourselves to death by
the violence of our own emotions.

Anyone who allows himself to be too long or too much
interested in any objective matter will find his powers
waning and his mind tending toward imbalance. The
neuroticism of our modern age is due to nothing so much
as to man's failure to know and to obey the law of the
Sabbath. The mind too much absorbed in the phenomenal world may easily fall into the pattern of becoming first
a crank and then a psychotic. Insanity is nature's benevo-
lence in withdrawing and detaching us from the problem
world when we either will not or do not know how to
detach ourselves and keep the Sabbath. In fact, we could
say that all pain is a means by which nature forces upon
us an unconscious observance of the Sabbath law. Pain
deflects our attention from those interests and movements
which caused it. A sufferer from a painful disease generally loses all consciousness of it on becoming deranged.
A disorder of the mind replaces the disorder of the body.
And, in an opposite manner, a disorder of the mind either
conscious or unconscious will gradually lead to some disorder of the body. An individual life always continues
happily and unimpaired so long as the individual can
choose between good and evil. But when this faculty is
impaired or if it remains undeveloped, then when the individual allows his mind to become involved in the strains
and tensions of the objective side of life, pains and physi-

cal disturbances follow. It is as if nature had no other means to deflect the mind. Thus out of sickness oftentimes comes a great illumination, a transfiguration of the personality, so that the whole course of the individual's life is changed from that point on.

A person who overworks or who is inordinately ambitious is building up for a violent reaction from the unconscious side of his life. When this reaction appears as bodily impairment or mental derangement or total apathy, he and his friends may consider it as a tragedy. It will really be the action of divine love withholding him from his purpose, endeavoring to turn his mind away from his obsession. If man will not voluntarily seek inquiry and meditation, he must be made to seek it by involuntary experience. The law of sleep and rest is a law of divine providence, tempering the wind to the shorn lamb, preventing us from wearing ourselves out in the conceited belief that we can solve the problems of the world without divine aid.

The Sabbath is designed to weaken or break the hold of the world upon us, to pare down our haughty confidence in our own self-sufficiency. A man is prostrated by disease. How rapidly all his worldly interests sink in value. A loved one is in danger or in need. How suddenly and relatively unimportant become money and all worldly possessions. When we are in extremity, all the world's pomp and vanity shrink in value and importance. In sleep they disappear entirely. If a man will meditate upon the Great Law and condition his mind to the truth by prayer, he will avoid the necessity for nature's corrective techniques. He will voluntarily return in his thinking and in his acting to the Sabbath rest and so obviate the need for any disease or corrective pain.

> I gave them my Sabbath to be a sign between me
> and them that they might know that I am the Lord
> that sanctify them.

The whole purpose of the Sabbath is to make men conscious of God, to develop in man an awareness of the spiritual world and the importance of thought and emotion as preceding the creation of physical experience. The Sabbath is not mere physical repose and functional recuperation. It is not idleness of body and of mind. It is not just interruption of the process of living. It is part of the living process. The Sabbath is a means of enlarging man's productive activities and increasing his joy in living. For only in the practice of the Sabbath law of detachment can he break the bondage of the senses and deliver himself from the thralldom of daily cares.

As we have seen, the nature of the physical world is continual flux and change. If a man's mind is too long absorbed in the physical world he becomes a victim of this world's moods. The world puts a ring in his nose and leads him around like a bull. His emotions are subject to all the changes that take place round about him. Ambitions drive him, conditions frustrate him, wars and rumors of wars keep him upset, competition worries him, disease threatens him, the prospect of old age and the uncertainties of the future eat away at his spirit. Every report of change in world conditions alternately encourages and depresses him. Like a barometer he reflects the weather around him. The men who have the capacity of establishing their own mental and spiritual climate are those who study and follow the Great Law and the injunction of the Sabbath is of the greatest help in achieving this stability. Man's spirit cannot find rest in the changing conditions of the outer world where there is no point of rest. There is no dry land which the waves of the world's emotion do not at some time inundate.

Yet man must needs live in the world and meet all these changes in order to realize the sovereignty of his own soul. In order to do this, however, he is forced by the law of his own nature to go back at certain intervals into the absolute nature of himself and walk and talk with his God, that he may be reminded of his spiritual sovereignty, that he may know again the infirmity and passing nature of all things mortal and created. For as Paul says, "He that is entered into his rest, he also hath ceased from his own works as God did from his." That is, he has ceased to struggle and strain with brain and body to make things come to pass without superior guidance, and has learned to search his own consciousness and to allow the law of God to manifest itself for him in his life. The people who followed Moses through the wilderness for forty years could not enter into the promised land because they could not observe the Lord's rest. They believed not the promises of God because they were fascinated by the evidences of their senses. "Let us labor therefore to enter into that rest, lest any man fall after the same example of unbelief." (Paul)

There is yet further evidence that the Sabbath is a universal and mathematically exact law of the nature of men and things, and that lies in the significance of the number seven itself. Ancient thinkers invested this number with a dignity and authority beyond all others. In the words of Philo of Alexandria:

> I doubt, whether any one could adequately celebrate the properties of the number seven, for they are beyond all words.

Something divine and beyond human thinking happens where the number seven is concerned. In the most ancient of all Chinese writings, the *I Ching,* a book already old in the days of Confucius, there is a passage which reads:

> By the constant return of the seventh day we may discern the mind of heaven.

There are very good reasons why people in all ages have sensed the significance of this magic number. Nearly everyone is familiar with the solar spectrum. A beam of sunlight passes through the beveled edge of a piece of glass and is broken up into its constituent elements of varying wave lengths, long waves at the top, short waves at the bottom. The resulting colors which are split up out of the beam of white light are seven in number. They are red, orange, yellow, green, blue, indigo and violet. In reverse order, when these colors are blended, they form a white light. So that one might say we make a complete circle from white light to white light by going through the number seven. In music, we can also see the functioning of seven. The diatonic scale which has been the basis of harmony of Western music for the past five centuries consists of seven different tones. The eighth tone, or octave, is the same as the first note in the scale.

In ancient times to swear or to take an oath meant to seven oneself. Outwardly this meant to repeat a promise or vow seven times. But of course this is not the real meaning. Actually to seven oneself is to gather all one's moods and thoughts together into an integration of consciousness which is confidence and rest, keeping no mental reservation, hiding no duality of purpose. Such a gathering of the forces of mind and emotion is a guarantee of performance and thus is called an oath.

We cannot leave the number seven without observing the remarkable properties of the number itself. There are only nine numbers which, with an added zero, are called the decad or the ten. Among these ten, only seven is a number of rest. It neither works nor is it the product of work. Or, as the ancients said of it, it neither begets nor is it begotten. The number one begets all the subsequent numbers while it is begotten by none whatever. Eight is made by twice four, but itself produces no number within the decad. Four both begets and is begotten. It begets eight by being doubled and is begotten by twice two. Number seven alone remains motionless. It is called the motherless virgin. The Pythagoreans called the number seven the chief of all things and likened it to the sovereign of the universe. Philolaus, a Pythagorean philosopher of the fifth century B.C. said:

> There is a supreme ruler of all things, God, ever one, abiding without motion, himself (alone) like unto himself, different from all others.

"Exempt from movement and from passion," as Philo of Alexandria describes it, the number seven is the symbol and the principle of all those who have great peace because they "love the law and nothing shall offend them." Its rule and sway can be noted everywhere in nature, in things visible and invisible, reminding and inspiring us at intervals of six stages to keep the seventh one holy.

CHAPTER FIVE

Honor the Source

**HONOUR THY FATHER AND THY MOTHER:
THAT THY DAYS MAY BE LONG UPON
THE LAND WHICH THE LORD THY GOD
GIVETH THEE.**

O N THIS EARTH WE RECEIVE LIFE through and by our parents. From father and mother come constitution, disposition and temperament of the child. The atmosphere of the home and the relationship between parents and children are transmuted into the personality factors of the offspring. Every child is a sensitive receiving instrument, faithfully recording the moods of its environment. The child who comes welcomed and desired into a home which abounds in love and assurance has a head start over those who are born into an atmosphere of strife and fear. Yet no person who is born into the latter condition should ever despair in later years and weakly blame his condition upon his parents and his early environment. By true spiritual knowledge he can overcome any handicap and even up the race between himself and the more highly endowed of his brothers and sisters.

When we come to the purely spiritual or psychological interpretation of this commandment we shall see that every person comes from a divine source and the working knowledge of this lifts him above the influence and effect of his environment past and present.

But right now we are dealing with the purely physical fact, a fact which confronts us all on the human plane of existence whether we have spiritual knowledge or not. As children we are all without the developed capacity of self-direction; hence we are moved upon and activated by the moods, sensations and suggestions of our surroundings. A child's soul registers fear before it is able to understand what fear is. The anxiety of the mother and the frustration of the father are readily communicated to the child's soul because it has no means of rejecting. The child's mind does not know the First Commandment, that there is only one power, and therefore cannot reason spiritually. That is, it has no means of comparing the knowledge and moods which it receives from others with the wisdom which it has within itself.

On the positive side, there are the love and protection and assurance and other sustaining communications from parents to child which cause the child to flourish and grow physically, mentally and emotionally. In fact, were it not for these positive values, no child would ever reach maturity. In recent years the prescription of a certain discerning physician in this connection has become the subject of universal admiration and approval. The physician wrote on the hospital chart of a little baby the following: "This baby to be loved every three hours." God is the Ever-living One and God is love; therefore love is life. We owe our lives to the love of our parents, therefore, the Fifth Commandment bids us to honor our father and our mother.

In the beginning our parents are God to us. In our early ignorance of spiritual causes, we have only the sense evidence to judge by. Hence we infer that our parents are our causes. We emerge from them, body and mind. They care for us, feed us and protect us. It is a rudimentary emotion to love our benefactors, just as the dog loves the hand that feeds it. In this play and interplay of love in the parent-child relationship, "standeth God within the shadow keeping watch upon His own." The undeveloped mind cannot possibly understand this formless, faceless God who works behind the shadow. A child's whole intelligence is geared to the perception of external form and sound and the sensation of these and it is not yet ready to comprehend what is beyond and above these. Thus do our parents stand for God in the early days and, so far as our basic human experience is concerned, they are God. If we can intelligently honor the human instruments of this supreme power, we shall in time be led to the understanding and proper honor of the Supreme itself.

Where the child is given love and is taught to return love, an integrated life will develop. But if love is withheld by the parents and ignorance and selfishness rule in the home, the child may grow up feeling no warmth of love toward its progenitors. In fact it may develop hate. This in turn will breed inferiority and other complexes which will mar the later life and happiness of the individual. It is a requirement of human happiness that we honor and love the source from which we spring.

Happy is that man or woman who can look to his parents with gratitude, respect and honor. For such movements of mind and feeling will develop confidence and self-respect and will furnish the fullest use of all one's faculties and powers. Without a healthy respect for one's parents, one's abilities are circumscribed and one's effectiveness diminished. Let no one say that he can find nothing in his parentage to respect and to honor. There is something in the poorest and meanest of parents for the child to seek out and to honor. Even if it is nothing more than the wonder and marvel of that mystery of nature which impels mothers, both animal and human, to a tender and fierce solicitude for their young—whether it is a bird seeking a protected place for her nest, a lioness savagely defending her young or a Nancy Hanks (in a poet's imagination) coming back from the grave to inquire if her son, Abe Lincoln, got to town, and how did he get on.

One can say, of course, that the maternal instinct is no credit to human intelligence, it is purely involuntary and instinctive and therefore compelled by the hand of the Infinite One. This is quite true, but if we cannot understand the infinite love in its human expressions and pay proper respect and honor to these human instruments, we shall never be able to understand the Infinite in its higher categories of expressions. Thus the Fifth Commandment, like all of the others, fits all levels of understanding and applies to every mind at every stage in its development.

"Honour thy father and thy mother: that thy days may be long upon the land which the Lord thy God giveth thee." That is, honor thy father and thy mother not alone because it is a moral or ethical law, or because society thinks it is good that you do so, or because it is an act of charity toward the old folks. It is much more than any or all of these together. It is a natural law of your being. You will honor your mother and father that you may be healthy and happy in your life here. The mind and soul which cannot find something to honor in the source from which it came will be miserable to the extent to which it failed in this regard.

Note that the more the child develops in understanding, the more he appreciates his parents. Many a boy or a girl who at eighteen was sure his parents were old fuddy-duddies, is amazed at twenty-five to discover how much the old folks have improved. Every age has its horse-and-buggy aspects and its atomic fringe. The lessons to be learned from life are not different when one rides in an airplane powered by a jet engine from those lessons which were to be learned when one rode in a two-wheel cart drawn by a donkey. The merchandise of life is always the same. It is only the window dressing that changes.

It is simply enlightened self-interest to honor one's father and one's mother. The consciousness always appropriates the qualities it admires or fears. Your emotional accent determines what you gather and what you reject out of life's offerings. You will become like that which you secretly love, and will draw strength and sustenance from that which you worship supremely.

A certain widow understood this principle when she was left with a house full of children of different ages. She took in washing and was hard put to feed and clothe and discipline her houseful of offspring. But she had a novel and effective way for inspiring perfect conduct. To little Mary she would say, "Mary, tell the truth and shame the devil, the way your father always did." And to Johnny she would say, "Johnny, wipe your feet when you come into the house, as your father always did." Now someone had known that her husband had been a drunkard and a wastrel and asked the woman why she held him up before the children as a paragon of virtue when he was anything but that. She replied that all the time that she was married to him he had never done a lick of work or aided in any way in the support of the family. "So," she said, "when he died I resolved that I was going to put him to work and make him help me raise this family."

The woman had a sound psychology. Every child should be told over and over again that he springs from a good source. This is where fear and inferiority are nipped in the bud, and self-esteem and self-respect are built into the foundation of the character. The Fifth Great Word recognizes that children should be taught to respect and honor their parents (regardless of faults) for the sake of their own health and happiness. It is in such an atmosphere that integrated lives develop and flourish. To the child the source of love and wisdom are his parents. He cannot yet be aware of the true God, so he must perforce worship the only God he knows or can know. So the first lesson is to teach him to honor his mother and father. If this is done wisely, the child will be led by easy steps to the true worship of the true God, the Most High, the parent of us all. For with the coming of spiritual maturity we shall all learn that our human parents are not our progenitors; that there is only one creative cause throughout all the world and throughout all time, one progenitor of all things, one God, one Father.

This represents a high point in spiritual learning, but before one reaches this peak the practice of the Fifth Commandment leads the developing soul up to two lower levels of spiritual integration and maturity. One of these, self-respect and self-confidence, we have already discussed. The second level of realization which everyone must reach is called obedience. The Fifth Commandment is designed to establish obedience in the unfolding individual. Obedience is a natural law in all human experience. "Nature obeys man in proportion as man first obeys Nature." Nature locks great power in the atom, but if man would make use of that power for his own expansion, he must first of all obey the laws of the atom. That mind which has not learned obedience cannot learn direction and command. If you would be warmed by the sun you must give yourself to the sun. If you would hear beautiful music, you must go where the music is and lend an ear. If you would hear what your friend says, you must give him your attention. If you would receive blessing or profit from anything, you must give it your mind.

In the higher reaches of spiritual maturity the act of giving becomes the mode of life. The great people of the world are ever the givers. They put the rest of the world in their debt. Giving implies possession, and all giving, whether in terms of money, time or expression of talent, first of all demands the giving of oneself, that is, one's attention, one's reference and deference to values which were once above him.

Every culture has had its way of saying that the gods come out of the heavens to dwell on earth with the men who worship them. The Christmas story is the account of God who became man. A psychological or metaphysical way of saying this is to say that those values and qualities which your mind honors, respects and worships are daily becoming more embodied in your individual and personal expressions. "Draw nigh unto him and he will draw nigh unto you." One must give himself to God and God will give himself to the individual. One cannot give or express what one does not possess. The way to acquire what you do not now own, is to give yourself to the consideration of it. There are all degrees of consciousness, and the lower receives from the higher and the higher descends into the lower. The lower is obedient to the higher and the higher commands the lower. There is always something above you, as there is always something below you. To increase the domain of your personal sovereignty, you must become a better servant to values which are presently above you. "Let him who would be first among you, become your servant." (Jesus) A great musician is a slave to his instrument and its principles and laws, but he commands the harmonies and rules the sensations of millions who listen to his playing.

The Fifth Commandment is a recognition of all of this and much more besides. The child who is brought up to honor and to obey his parents will early have the quality of obedience integrated into his character. In his adult life he will not find it difficult to adapt to the demands of business and professional routine. He will not find the law of the land restrictive, or family duties irksome. His frustrations will be fewer, and his successes will be easier and greater. In other words, he will grow up and become a spiritual adult, especially if he can take one more step, which the Fifth Commandment points to, on the road to spiritual maturity. That next step is the awareness of the true Father, of whom our parents were but childhood's representations.

The Fifth Great Word in the decalogue bids us honor father and mother for the sake of our own self-development and maturity, so that we may be led intelligently and step by step to that true and proper honor, which belongs to God and God alone. At this point is born the consciousness that flesh and blood have never fathered anything; that the true, creative power or father is spirit, known to us as mind and consciousness. "Call no man on earth your father," says Jesus, "for one is your Father, which is in heaven." Heaven means the nonphysical or the immaterial realm, which can only be mind or consciousness, or the un-formed realm behind mind and consciousness, which is spirit.

Physically, you may trace your origin back to the sperm and ovum of your father and your mother, but will you stop there? The sperm and the ovum are just little pieces of protoplasm. How and wherein do they contain the qualities and the characteristics of the person which pro-ceeds from them? Still reasoning biologically, you might say that your qualities and characteristics come through the genes and chromosomes which you inherit equally from father and mother through the sperm and the ovum. Physical science locates the characteristics of the individual in the chromosomes, but this is only carrying your biologi-cal origin back a step further. You are still dealing with matter when dealing with the genes and chromosomes. The point to consider is how your individual temperament and disposition and your particular nervous patterns are implanted and contained in the genes which you inherit from your father and your mother. Certainly the single cell from which all of our physical being emerges is the great mystery of life. In it somehow is contained the union of the spiritual and the physical. In this single cell is the pattern of our body, the color of our eyes and hair, the peculiar and particular bent of our mind and the individ-ual complex of moods and feelings which will dominate our temperament.

The consciousness of the parents is implanted in the cell from which the child grows. Not only the body but the mind as well begins in this single cell. It is mind in and as our parents which has fathered us. It is mind in and as the matter of the first cell which gave us our beginning. At conception the basic mental patterns of our father and our mother were bequeathed to us. Our basic temperament, constitution, vitality and personality bent were established at this point.

From this point on in the growth of a new life until the child has grown and developed its own reasoning powers and is able to take some conscious, volitional part in the direction of its own thinking, it is largely under the governance of the consciousness of its parents. To some extent, of course, every mental and emotional influence in the child's environment qualifies it and affects it and modifies its growth and development. When the child goes to school, the teacher will take over a part of the job of influencing its development. From all of its contacts with the outside world it will receive some impressions.

As Quimby used to say, every newborn child is like a tablet upon which everyone who comes along does a little scribbling, but the parents are the controlling factors. There is a rapport between parents and child which is never completely broken. Over this as over a telephone wire the moods of the parents are transmitted to the child. The bickerings and the fears, as well as the joys and the assurances, travel from parent to child and are woven into the personality structure. When the child develops and it begins to think for itself, it assumes a part of its own mental direction. It begins to reason, to react to outside impressions and to make decisions and act upon them. But the suggestion of maturity and freedom in this transition of mental action from parent to child may be an illusion. From the standpoint of spiritual goals, certainly from the standpoint of the practical goals of health and happiness, the child may be no further along than he was before. His spiritual development will depend on the only actor in this whole drama of life—mind or consciousness.

In this phase we are here considering, the scene of action has shifted from parent to offspring, but the kind of thinking may not be changed. For example, father and mother feared colds every time the weather changed. They were slaves to the belief that weather changes could produce sickness in their child. Their fears conditioned the child. Now that the child is more or less on his own he has these same fears. He fears weather changes and acts like a slave or a primitive in his futile efforts to ward off the effect of weather on his breathing apparatus. He is unaware that much of the cause of his affliction is in himself, buried deep in his subjective depths, left there long ago by the influences of his environment before he ever began to think consciously about these things. The child may have become a physical adult, but mentally and emotionally he is still as he was when a child, dependent and without any strong rudder with which to steer a self-chosen course. He is indeed removed from his father's house, he is far from parental environment and influence, but the parental mind still lives and flourishes in him. Spiritually he has not grown up. He is still too close to what Jesus calls the "world"—that peculiar primitive state of mind which sees gods in air and fire and sticks and stones, and material causation everywhere. "Saying to a stock, Thou art my father; and to a stone, Thou hast brought me forth." (Jeremiah 2:27)

Spiritual maturity means a change in one's whole thinking. One must some time discover the spiritual principle of mind and consciousness as the one, true Father and then he will "Call no man on earth his Father." He will no longer blindly accept the conditioning and the influencing of his path and say by way of explanation of his defeats and his misery, "I am a victim of my training. If I were trained differently I would be different." Discovering the mind principle, he will no longer attribute to environment a power which it does not possess. He will learn that no person, no situation, no thing, has any power to influence the mind of man except in and through the reaction of that mind. To a mind that does not react, there is no effect, no movement, no authority, no result. One must at some time in his existence "leave the world" with Jesus, and "go unto the Father." That is, go unto the true cause and progenitor of all expression and experience. If the child has been rightly taught to honor the cause in all things beginning with his father and mother, to seek for the cause of all action, to be scientific in this seeking and not just to accept the opinions and the platitudes of others, he will be led naturally and step by orderly step through all the phases of childhood and immaturity, to the spiritual realization of the Father in heaven or the cause in mind.

This is the great accomplishment toward which the whole Bible points. Its whole purpose is to bring the individual out of the general or world mind into that particular revelation which is called Christ, which is a saved state, because it is freedom from the thralldom and misery of the world-mind. If one understands this, he is, according to the Christian doctrine, "baptized," that is, washed and cleansed from the taint of the world-mind. He has "come out from among them," and lives an entirely new life of freedom and joy which cannot be known under the old dispensation. He is no longer under the bondage of the law, but lives in the freedom and in the joy of his wisdom. He knows that this law of bondage was not a law imposed from without, but was the law of his own thinking as his thinking was based upon false premises. It is this freedom of the individual and this sovereignty of the spiritual principle within the individual that Jesus came to teach. "For one is your Father," he says, "which is in heaven." It was a spirit, a consciousness, which generated you. You are spirit, a phase of the whole spirit. Because you are spirit, the generating principle is within you. Therefore you as an individual can regenerate, taking hold of the same principle which generated you in the beginning. If you do not like what you now are, you are not limited by the past. You are free by the knowledge which you possess of the generating principle to change your thought, mind, consciousness, and therefore change your body and your environment. You need not fear environment any longer. Dropping your fear of things and people and conditions, your true spirit or desire is no longer stymied or inhibited and is therefore free to move in confidence and in faith, to execute itself, to embody itself in your world and bring you the joy that can come only from this movement of life from the inside to the outside. Outwardly it looks as though you are limited by your conditioning, by your parents' frailties, by all the fears and vexatious emotions which you inherited, by the impressions which you gather from your environment about you. But with your knowledge that consciousness is the Father, you are free and able to move steadily ahead.

Every man, then, has a higher Source than his physical parents. The understanding of this is the second level to which the Fifth Commandment calls the mind. "Look unto the rock, whence you are hewn . . ." (Isaiah 51:1) By such looking one is led in good order and systematically into that spiritual maturity which transfers its allegiance from physical causation to spiritual causation. This spiritual maturity and this transfer of attention and allegiance is indicated in the story of Jesus talking to the people, while his mother and his brethren stood without, desiring to speak with him.

> Then one said unto him, Behold, thy mother and thy brethren stand without, desiring to speak with thee. But he answered and said unto him that told him, Who is my mother? and who are my brethren?

> And he stretched forth his hand toward his disciples,
> and said, Behold my mother and my brethren! For
> whosoever shall do the will of my Father which is in
> heaven, the same is my brother, and sister, and
> mother. (Matthew 12:47)

At spiritual maturity, life is newly interpreted in terms
of the mind and the spirit. Spiritual maturity has for its
following and its kin every constructive thought anywhere
and everywhere. And every constructive emotion which
flows from your new kind of thinking is the mother of
your new experience. The spirit is always the father, but
the thoughts and moods of my own consciousness are the
womb in which the new phases of my being and experience are ever taking shape. Whatever constructive thought
and emotion does the will of my Father in heaven, that is,
establishes peace and confidence in me and helps every
true desire into being and expression, the same is my
mother and my brethren.

The Fifth Commandment bids us pay honor to earthly
mother and father that we may at last be led to perceive
the true mother and father of consciousness. Or, read from
a higher point of view, this commandment encourages one
to pay supreme honor to the true parents of mind and
spirit that our days may be long and happy in this land,
in this life.

Don't (try) to kill the power

THOU SHALT NOT KILL

THIS IS THE HALFWAY POINT of the Ten Words. If the Ten Commandments are represented by an open book, then this point is the binding of the book which unites the two halves. For at this point we pass from the realm of subjective activity to the arena of objective action. We are moving from thought. We are in the midpassage of the Jordan, having passed through the wilderness of the human mind's confusion and wandering, having fought and having been fought with. Always having followed the gleam of hope, the promise of the voice of God within us, and having perfected ourselves in the use of the law which He has handed down to us, we now at last find ourselves at the place of crossing over into the Promised Land.

All our hopes and dreams and expectations were promises until now. At this point they become realized as facts and functions. Here they receive bodies and garments, here thoughts are made things. The first Five Words were

all related to the realm of thought, mind and consciousness. These first five were all pertinent directions of the
movements of our own thoughts and feelings within ourselves. The second five set forth the expression of these
thoughts and feelings, or the embodiment of the mind's
contents.

The left-hand tablet is called the Law because it is
concerned with establishing the Divine Law in the mind.
In meditating upon the first Five Words we are con-
strained to let go of many of our negative concepts and
to embrace more positive and helpful ones. The mind is
weaned away from its false allegiance to many outside
forces and brought to a conviction of one power as the
sole and only cause of all expression, action and function.
When this condition is established in any individual mind,
that mind can then be said to be a prophet or a predictor
of the good things to come. Thus, the right-hand tablet is
called the Prophets, for it foretells human action which is
the result of thought or consciousness.

Regardless of what its philosophy may be, every mind
predicts its own future and casts its own shadow before
it and in that sense is a prophet of things to come. With
the philosophy of the first Five Words firmly established
in the thinking and willing of the human mind, that mind
becomes a prophet of God. That is, it prophesies in its
continual thinking and meditating the attainment of the
things of life that come only of God's doing. The individual's life then is seen to be the expression of God's will. A
prophet always speaks for God and announces God's will

in earthly matters. The action life of a person, represented by the second tablet, is such a prophet. Hence, we have the tablets called The Law and The Prophets.

Since all human action is really reaction, what a person says or does is foreordained by what he has thought or meditated upon. As a man thinketh in his heart so is he and so does he. Our choice is in the realm of ideas; our actions are compulsory. Men imagine so often that they are free when actually they are the bond servants of the ideas they have lived with. The alcoholic, for example, who will not yet accept the fact that he is an alcoholic imagines that he is free and that he can "take it or leave it." His feeling that he is free and that he has the ability to choose comes from the potentiality, which he has not yet realized, speaking within him.

Every person is, potentially and in principle, free, but principle and function are two different things. In principle I am potentially an aviator because I am a man, and men can fly. But in actual practice I would require many hours, perhaps years, of thinking and practice with the principles of aviation before I could actually fly. A little talent in any direction and a clear understanding of this principle of freedom and there is no limit to what a person can achieve. Instead of bucking the world and fighting for his place in the sun against the competition of other beings, he can think and meditate his way into place and by such meditation invoke such powerful divine energies that they shall compel him into good as formerly their opposites have compelled him into error. Man's rulers are

in his mind and every man chooses his rulers. In its ignorance the average mind comes under the sway of the
despots and tyrants of the world-mind, falls unwilling victim to sickness, misfortune and want. The Bible forever
points to the kingdom of God or, as we say in the New
Testament, the kingdom of Christ, which means God
within man. Paul speaks of being a prisoner of Jesus
Christ and therefore in bondage to no man and to no
limitation. Despots rule by the ignorance of the people,
their victims. When that ignorance is displaced by spiritual wisdom the power of the despot is broken.

The artist Abner Dean has portrayed this truth very
well in one of his discerning cartoons. He shows a haughty
figure on the high end of a teeter-totter and an abject
suppliant on the low end. No words, no caption. The picture itself is a sermon on the life of man. The only power
there is, is in man himself. In his ignorance he gives away
this power and elevates his enemies over and above himself. If those who sit in darkness should see the great light
and their eyes be once unveiled, they will look around
them, understand their condition, move from their place
and let their tormentor fall to the ground.

Thus when the Great Law in its Sixth Word announces
that thou shalt not kill, it means essentially that you shall
not kill the life or the real being in yourself. I say that
this is its primary meaning, because all external killing
is the reactive mechanism of internal self-murder. No man
ever lifted his hand in violence against his brother without
first having lifted his hand against himself in his own

thought. All crime is but the expression of internal discord. Our civil law defines first-degree murder as the culminating physical confirmation of premeditation and malice aforethought. The mind is a unity, but its thoughts, attitudes and moods can be like a happy family or like a den of thieves. When the parts of the mind do not agree, inner warfare sets in and there is murder in the temple and spilling of blood in the holy place. In other words, the mind which should be the sanctuary of God, the dwelling place of peace and quiet power, confidence and joy, is at war with itself and is foolishly killing off its finer parts.

If a mind becomes angry, it kills reason and good sense. If a mind becomes fearful, it kills courage and confidence. When a mind is jealous and vengeful, it is strangling hope and destroying faith. When a mind turns to bitterness, it has pulled down the shades on vision and is blindly bent on its own destruction. Constantly in our society these internal commotions are being precipitated outwardly into form and function and that makes the crime in the world. To kill means to remove from consciousness. Any state of consciousness, therefore, that culminates in a person's taking the life of another person is an emotion which has already killed something in the murderer.

The Great Law says that there is only one Being, completely in harmony with itself. If you, as an individual, look outward and see something or someone opposed to your desires and purposes, you are giving existence to "another" in your mind. When you quarrel with it in the

mind and think and feel violently toward it, you are trying hard to kill or overcome your opposition. But since
opposition is an illusion, a temporary obstacle in the mind
that right thinking can solve, you are really killing something in yourself. You are devitalizing yourself and destroying the power to live. Should these angry emotions
continue for any length of time, you will find yourself
compelled to take some violent action externally toward
others.

Any one who kills has a consciousness of limitation. In
his ignorance he thinks to remove the limitation. The
gunman who holds up a store and kills the man behind
the counter in order to rifle the till, is only acting out the
little drama of his own mind. He desires money because
he desires food, clothes, drink or entertainment, not knowing that he could have any and all of these things on the
basis of his own consciousness and effort. He, it may be,
believes that others who have these things are holding
them away from him; that he is the victim of conditions;
that society is against him and he must fight his way to
freedom. His concepts form the opposition in his mind to
his desires. But when he walks into the store, it is the
storekeeper who is, in his eyes and understanding, the opposition or the antagonist between him and the money
which he wants. All subjectivity is projected into objec-
tivity, either rationally or irrationally. So he kills the man
behind the counter and thinks that he has removed his
opposition. And so he has, in the little drama that is being
enacted in that moment. But this little drama is with a

reduced cast and is only one small scene from the whole. Actually the gunman has slain himself or a part of himself. In allowing himself to become the victim of an irrational desire and passion he has wounded good reason and good sense, pushed himself further away from the possibility of right action and right results. He has given himself into the mastery of a devil which will sooner or later destroy him completely. He goes first to prison or to the gallows in himself, and then later he will meet with society's confirmation of this.

In the early pages of the Bible we read that Cain rose up and slew his brother Abel. The casual and superficial reader will suppose that he understands this, that an actual man has been slain by another actual man. But the careful reader of that psychological drama which is our Bible, the story of man in his entirety, will descern that Cain and Abel, being brothers, represent the two parts of a single individual. Cain is self-will and human reason. Abel is recognition of and deference to a divine will and a divine standard. Abel is the beginnings of spiritual reason based upon an understanding of the Great Law. These two modes of action are in us all. In the ordinary man, ignorant of spiritual things, Cain always slays Abel. This does not mean that Abel as a being is utterly destroyed, extirpated and banished from the realm of being. It simply means that this constructive mode of thinking is abolished from the mind of the human fool. It is dethroned from consciousness and plunged into unconsciousness. It is a psychological death, but not a destruction. It is all a commentary again upon the oneness of being and an explanation of the fact that when any person thinks he kills another he is really destroying himself psychologically. His life is one slow, long series of little deaths culminating finally in some physical death by violence, usually. Genesis says that the Lord set a mark upon Cain lest any finding him should kill him. "The Lord said unto him, therefore whosoever slayeth Cain, vengeance shall be taken on him sevenfold." In other words, whoever fights evil upon its own plane in an effort to destroy it, far from destroying he increases it by his handling of it. "Resist not evil, but overcome evil with good." (Jesus) A more illuminating translation of this passage in Genesis is, I think, the one which reads: "Whosoever killeth Cain shall raise him sevenfold." In our common language we have an expression about "raising Cain" by which we refer to violence and noise and all inconsiderate self-action. Whoever tries to fight evil becomes like it and magnifies its qualities in himself.

Modern metaphysical science teaches us not to try to solve a problem on its own plane or level. The law of suggestion and psychic influence is always operative and we become the victims of that to which we give our attention—good, if it be good; bad, if it be bad. The leader of the vice squad must be changed frequently lest he, himself, become engaged in the evils he seeks to arrest. Nurses and doctors who specialize in or who work too long with the same fearsome diseases need a Sabbath from their work lest they give birth in themselves to that which they are trying to destroy. Evil in all of its forms is not destructible. No man can destroy it. As the Lord says, no one can destroy Cain. He can raise it into consciousness or plunge it into unconsciousness. It is sufficient for the good man to know this and to know how to do it. Everybody encounters evil; it is a necessary part of the growth to maturity.

So when the Great Law says thou shalt not kill, it is but reaffirming the prayer process announced in each of the other Ten Words. It is saying that you should keep the temple of your consciousness clean of all beliefs in antagonistic forces in the sense-world, and honor in your heart of hearts one presence and one power from whom and by whom are all things and acts. There is nothing and no one in the sensible world who can hurt you without your permission. Therefore, there is nothing in the created world to fear. Give power to no external conditions, to no person, and you are delivered from the necessity of feeling angry or resentful, or peeved or remorseful, but encouraged to hope and be confident. All your true desires can and will find happy fulfillment through the law of God. These truths are of God, and if they live in your soul then you are alive in God, which is a way of saying that you are alive in good reason and in good sense. Not having murdered the truths of life within yourself you will be under no compulsion to murder any living being in the outside world. Since you no longer project your own unreasonable attitudes or imperfect conceptions outwardly on to other people, you will discover that people are better than you knew and find it in your heart to love your neighbor as yourself. For the love you bear toward those true and heavenly parts of yourself is the measure of that love that you are able to bestow upon others who are but the external extension of yourself. "Whoso sheddeth man's blood, by man shall his blood be shed: for in the image of God made he man." (Genesis 9:6)

All of the foregoing is pertinent to the subject of one person killing another. But what about the person who is killed? What about the storekeeper who was shot down by the bandit? What about the innocent victim of an automobile accident?

First of all, accident is a word we use to describe an event, the causes of which we do not know or which are unseen. Yet it is self-evident that every event must have its cause or causes. No one knows the secrets of another's consciousness. All the heredity and environmental influences which have gone into the conditioning of our friends' consciousness are largely unknown to the rest of us. Even though the outside of a person's life is always conformable to the inside, there is a time lag between them, and we never fully know the state of the consciousness until we see the act. The Great Law teaches the regnancy of consciousness everywhere and at all times.

In the light of this Great Law no one dies save by his own hand. Granted that death is seldom the conscious choice of an individual, it is nevertheless the result of subjective or unconscious allowances. Everything that happens to us may be classified under one of these two heads: either we deliberately wooed the experience and the event by our self-conscious thinking and willing, or we subconsciously suffered it to happen to us by not denying and countering those influences which were pushing us in the direction of that experience. The world-mind is always pushing us. No one can live in this world without being subject in some measure to its fears and anxieties and its false beliefs. We live in a psychic sea which is made up of all the emotions of mankind, good and bad and indifferent. Every individual has telepathic and clairvoyant powers on the subjective level which put him constantly in touch with all other beings and things, whether he be conscious of it or not. By a process which may be likened to that of osmosis in the laboratory by means of which two liquids exchange places through a dividing membrane, we are constantly exchanging moods and ideas with all other people with whom we come in contact. That is why the ancient and proverbial dictum enjoins us to keep good company lest we go astray of right reason and right action.

The internal considerings of another human being are a little drama which none of us sees, yet it is this inner drama which determines the external performance which we later witness. The fears and anxieties and regrets and resentments of a person are the little deaths which build up into the culmination of what the world calls the final death. People sometimes assume because a man is "good" in the external sense—he goes to church, gives to charity, and is kind and gentle with others, industrious and dili-

gent of habit—that therefore it is a cruel injustice for death
to come to him, especially by some accident or cruel sickness. The good are not supposed to suffer. Yet we see
that all around us those who are judged to be good in the
highest sense often suffer the cruelest misfortune and pain,
while those who are called wicked seem always to ride the
crest of the wave of happiness and good health.

But external goodness is far different from internal
goodness. Internal goodness means the squaring of one's
thoughts and feelings with the knowledge of the Law.
Justice is squareness. Squareness means arranging the
processes of our lives in right-angled relationship with the
Great Law. This is goodness psychologically and spiritually speaking. Thus a man may be good in the traditional,
external sense and may be in error inwardly. His error
culminates in some trouble or sickness. This leads some
people to curse God, reject their religion and deny their
faith because, they suppose, these have denied them in
their plea for mercy. But we must remember that the
spiritual forces of life, which are emotional, are governed
by the thoughts of the mind, by reason, by spiritual or
right reason. If our convictions be erroneous, and the
premises of our reasoning are errors, then our thinking
processes do but evoke the evil forces of Pandora's box, or
our own unconscious. It is true we may do this in ignorance, so there is no blame attached. Nevertheless it is real
and actual. And we must understand it if we would be
delivered from it.

The mercy of God is sure and eternal and extended to

every living thing. In its vaster beneficence it must await the recognition and understanding of the individual. The showers from heaven are falling, but if we have no vessel to catch them, they will return in their circuit to the heavens and come again when, hopefully, we may be more receptive to them. The child has not yet developed a mind which can reason and think upon these things and so it is perforce under the governance of the reasoning of its parents and associates. If you have a little child living with you or near you, you cannot guess the great responsibility which is upon you. You are literally making that child in your image and your likeness. Not in the ideal image of your hope for that child, but in the imagery of your concepts of your own self, of the child and of all other people and all other things. For God made man in his image and likeness. To be like God is to be a creator. Since God created man in his own image, he must have created a being with powers like himself.

When calamity strikes we cannot place the blame upon any one or on any group of people. For we do not know what influences have conditioned the consciousness of the victims. Let us not argue and distress ourselves by fighting against God. There is one power and all things happen by that one power. Let us be satisfied with this. Let us know that this one power gives us all that we ask. It is our business to learn how to ask. Our sufferings are but the correctives which bid us ask more intelligently.

Be true to your idea

THOU SHALT NOT COMMIT ADULTERY

THIS COMMANDMENT, LIKE THE OTHER NINE, has its double meaning. First of all, it has its literal meaning which is more or less obvious to all. Experience has taught man that the marriage of one man with one woman living together in a family unit is the happiest and healthiest arrangement both for society and for the individuals. We need not marshall the evidence for this here.

One's too few; three too many.

When people find marriage restricting and confining, or vexing and burdensome, it is because they are restricted in their inner life. Externals are the projections of internals. "No man [manifestation] cometh unto me except the Father send him." (Jesus) To one who knows the spiritual law there can be no vexation or restriction in the marriage relationship. Moreover, love will flourish and not grow cold as it does when people's inner development does not keep pace with the needs of their environment.

Those who marry because they want another to compensate for a lack in themselves will always be disappointed in marriage. Trouble and pain always come in human life because of our insufficiency and our inadequacy. The sad thing is that sufficiency and adequacy are so near at hand and may be had for a little effort. Spiritually, we are always equipped for life. Intellectually, we do not know this. Our ignorance is our sin. And our sin is our disease and our pain. When man fell from his original spiritual state, the great truths of life sank into unconsciousness. They are there, awaiting resurrection. Man must mature and arise in the consciousness of these truths. There is a well deep in every man which, when tapped, will spring up into health and happiness if he will but dig long enough. The man who is not developed inwardly in regard to the truths of being is still a child, and the child must live by rules and under restrictions. The child must be forced to do certain things by rote. He must do them because he is told to do them, not because he can understand the reason why. But when he becomes of age he will see the reason and continue these right actions by choice.

So it is with everyone in regard to the rules and restrictions of society and law and order. They are often burdensome and vexatious to the immature mind. For those who are not spiritually developed, the Commandments are prohibitions and restraints upon their unredeemed instincts and passions. To those people who have found themselves inwardly the Ten Commandments are but guides, suggestions and reminders. They do not restrain or inhibit; they point the way to the green pastures and the still waters. They are the signposts on the way to freedom.

To those who have spiritual insight the Seventh Commandment is seen first of all to be a rule for the operations of the mind. If the workings of the mind be in divine order, then one's external relationships will also be in divine order in the same way that the cart follows the horse that draws it. With spiritual insight we see that it is the mind first of all which makes marriages, and the mind which breaks its marriage or adulterates its marriage cannot possibly find happiness in any human relationship. The mind marries ideas, opinions, concepts, theories.

Psychologically, your marriage partner is the idea, or concept, or goal, you love above all the world. When you pray, you are trying to make a marriage. When you are seeking any kind of good, you are endeavoring to join in union with a higher element of life. The essence of good prayer is very much like a love affair. All the period of courtship between a boy and a girl before marriage is very much illustrative of that process of mind by which we desire something, court it, work with it, think about it, meditate upon it and marry it to the imagination, until it becomes a living, working element in our daily lives. This is the law behind our institutions and our forms, and if one understands and practices this law he will find health and happiness and success. And since he finds these things he will hold no grudge against others. He cannot be bitter or angry. For a well man and a successful man has no reason for these emotions. Such a person is composed, magnanimous and charitable and so he satisfies all the rules of religion. His outer acts are in conformity with his inner rightness.

Thus the Great Law teaches us to get what we want through prayer, to apply the spiritual law and achieve good health and happiness and peace within ourselves. When this is accomplished we shall not have to worry unduly about our outer acts or expression. They will fade into the background because they are directed by a higher law.

When you are "in love" you cannot think of anything else. Lovers, notoriously, lose their appetite. Nothing is of interest but the one you love. It is like this with the mind. Your devotion must be whole-souled and supreme. The marriage service mentions that you have selected your partner out of all the world to be true to him or her alone. In the prayer process you cannot deal with a confusion of desires and purposes. You must come to the point. You must make a decision. You must clarify, select and set your course. Then you must give your attention to your purpose. If you are driving an automobile on a busy highway you must keep your eyes upon the road. You cannot with safety read all the billboards, turn your head and talk with the occupants in the back seat, or in general indulge a roving eye. "Keep on the beam," "Keep your eye on the ball"—these, and many other expressions like them, are always pointing out to us in our daily life that defin-

itiveness, decision and perseverance are the necessary ingredients of success. So you must love your goal, your
purpose in life, and be wholly devoted to it. Give it all of
your love. It requires that, if it is to come and live with
you.

Now the Great Law teaches in its corollaries that a person should not lie or cohabit with another—you shall not
dwell with another. When you keep your eyes upon your
goal you are thinking in terms of it and you are thereby
generating moods about it. When you turn your gaze
from the thing that you love you must of necessity occupy
your attention with something less desirable. What occupies your attention long enough will gradually build itself
up into a culmination or a climax and precipitate itself
into your physical world as some event or experience. The
adulteress, says Solomon (Prov. 6:26) hunts for the pre-
cious life. That is, the negative concept to which you give
attention will steal the force of your resolution. The
Seventh Commandment is another injunction about good
mental practice. Irrespective of your physical sex, your
wife is your conception, your conception of things in general and your conception of anything in particular. It is a
conception which you have espoused and with which you
will have to live so long as you are espoused to it. If you
give yourself to some great ideal you must give yourself
unreservedly to it and not allow extraneous details to creep
into your considerations. Doubt and hesitancy and inde-
cisiveness and fear and, of course, vexation with people
and situations, must not be allowed within the house of

your consciousness. These extraneous things are other wives with whom your mind is cohabiting. And in this act the mind is not loyal to its true wife, the ideal thing, which alone can mother the mind's true desires. What is called loyalty between man and wife on the physical plane is thus seen to be simply good order on the mental plane. Order is the law of all happy things. The devil is the author of confusion.

Suppose, for example, that you found a business. Only in exceptional instances do business projects succeed bountifully from the very beginning. There is usually a period of spadework and struggle requiring faith, diligence, good husbandry and perseverance. The conception of yourself as a successful businessman, your ideal of accomplishment and achievement—this is your wife. If you wish to succeed and be happy, be loyal to that wife. Give her everything you have, all the while expecting her to reciprocate. Do not take long vacations. Do not let others run your business while it is still weak and wobbly. Keep your eye on the accounts. See that your policy and yours alone governs in every aspect of the business. In other words, attend to the job at hand with the full confidence that you are living and working by a rule which brings inevitable success. If you follow this rule you cannot avoid being positive and constructive in all of your thoughts and dealings in your business and in your private life as well. Being thus confident that you are working with a great law which never fails, you will avoid the little doubts and apprehensions, gnawing worries and irritations that affect more unknow-

ing people. You will not adulterate your marriage. Thus
you will be true to your wife and she will be true to you.
She will mother your heart's desire, or bring you into the
position of having a flourishing business. You may have
the most wonderful ideal and the most brilliant idea.
These are the fathers of things to be, but they will remain
alone and unproductive until you find their marriage
partners. The marriage partner is the mood, the conception, the feeling, the enthusiasm, the inward mental work
which alone can give flesh and body to your ideals. Marry
your feeling to your idea and a third element enters, an
element which cannot be called by any other name than
God.

Every creative act in history, whether it was a master-
piece of engineering, invention or artistry, was accomplished by the marriage of the brain and the heart, the
thought and the feeling. These are the two parts of that
being called man. When these two come together on any
plane, a third is present, whose name is nameless, whose
form is formless and whose face cannot be seen by man.
"Where two or three are gathered together in my name,
there am I in the midst of them." (Jesus)

So you will see that the Seventh Word is trying to tell
you how to achieve right order and right action in your
own mind, implying that if you do this you will have no
trouble on the physical plane, for happy, healthful, successful people are God-led people. They do not break
their marriages. They make right marriages in the first

place. Once a person sees the divine law and puts it into practice in his life he is under a divine governance which is something like an automatic pilot in an airplane which keeps it on the course without human hands or brain in attendance. And that is one of the great reasons why the Master says, "Come unto me all ye that labor and are heavy laden, and I will give you rest." For only this knowledge of the Great Law active in your life can give you any real rest and relief from that increasing load of burdens which come to the unknowing mind, and which, without relief, will exhaust all human resources. Stick with your aim, love your ideal, do not allow the mind to cohabit with any other. To do so will bring only mixed or limiting results. "If thy right eye offend thee, pluck it out." If your objective perception offends your sense of peace and confidence, change it immediately. Cast off such a perception and return to your first love, and behold in her eyes the answer to all you hope and dream for.

If today you have great matters on your mind which need the help of God, then this evening should be devoted to prayer and treatment, to the invocation of the divine energy on behalf of those matters. It is better, then, that you lay aside the newspaper with its headlines of crime and violence, disappointment and thievery and all the emotions that attend upon the level of the unredeemed mind and heart of the race—it is better, much better, that you cut off this tendency to meddle with the world's sensations and enter into the heaven of prayer and union with

your good. In doing so you will achieve a future joy beyond description.

This Seventh Word calls other matters into mind such
as that of divorce, but this is not the place for a long discussion of this subject so I shall only speak briefly of the
one Biblical ground for divorce. You must distinguish
clearly between the Biblical meaning and that superficial
meaning which men often give to it. Many people suppose
that the Bible forbids divorce. This is not so. The New
Testament rule for divorce is as follows:

> Whosoever shall put away his wife, except it be
> for fornication, and shall marry another, committeth
> adultery. And whoso marrieth her which is put away
> doth commit adultery. (Matthew 19:9)

As we have seen throughout this book, there is no
understanding of any exterior human act or function save
in understanding the anterior and interior metaphysical
function which precedes it. Men have given to the word
fornication only a limited, external meaning. When a
married person becomes involved sexually with another
person, that is what men usually call fornication. Not so
with the Bible. The Bible is not directly concerned with
the physical event. It everywhere stresses the metaphysical
event. If a husband with a roving eye gets involved with
another woman on the physical plane, the Bible would
stress the fact that it was his roving eye which was his sin.
If a wife, through peevishness or weakness, or through the
neglect of her husband, becomes similarly involved in a tri-

angular relationship, the Bible again would stress the fact that it is her own weakness or slothfulness which is her sin rather than the physical event itself. Fornication, in the Biblical view, is the unlawful mental and emotional intercourse with ideas outside and extraneous to your announced and desired purpose in life. If it has appealed to your mind that one should live heathfully and happily and successfully in this life; that the kingdom of heaven is within; that as a spiritual being you can do something about every problem; that there is a principle within you which can raise you out of the average experience of the race where so much misfortune and illness are the common lot; that there is a way of prayer which is scientific and effectual—if this has appealed to your reason, you have embarked upon it as a way of life. You have married this concept, and it is just good sense to be loyal to it, to think it day and night, to perfect your understanding of it, to increase your experiences of it. Knowing that the subjective mind in you is responsive to every thought and word, tending to give you its embodiment or, as the Bible says, "A man shall give an account in the day of judgment of every idle word," you will be diligent in guarding your mind from the intrusion of all negative and limiting ideas and moods. If you come into contact with them you will greet them and pass on. You will not stop to chat or be invited in. In Biblical language, you will not lie down or cohabit with them. You will not give them your force nor partake in yourself of their vibrations. If, in your announced program of health and happiness and success in this daily life, you allow your mind to indulge in descriptions of evil, imaginations of loss or limitation, ruminations about illness or misfortune, or in any way cohabit with negation, you are guilty of the sin of fornication. And your sin is *ipso facto* divorce from your true marriage partner and the thing that you love above all else. You have broken your marriage. You have put away your real wife. That is, you have become neglectful and unconscious of her. She still resides in your unconscious depth. No man can put away his ideals entirely. But because she no longer has the attention of the conscious mind to encourage and nurture her, she becomes the unwilling victim of all the world's negation. Therefore, you have committed adultery in putting her away and in living with another. She has committed adultery because she is with others while belonging to you.

We have seen that unless we run our own subjective or emotional life, the world will run it for us and will impregnate it with all sorts of ideas of limitation. Every person must learn to run his own life with God-wisdom or he will become merely the hypnotic victim of the world thought about him. Our emotional life is always subservient to our reason or our intellectual life. When reason and good sense walk out of the house of the mind, then the emotional life is subject to intruders, burglars, rapists and murderers. If by the indulgence of bad habit you allow the mind to picture limitation rather than fullness of life, you have abandoned your true love, and that is *ipso facto* divorce.

Physical marriages are broken by this kind of mental action. For a person grows by thinking constructively, and he deteriorates by thinking negatively. When one thinks negatively continuously he meets reverses in life. His health wanes. He grows irritable, nervous, petulant, disagreeable. These moods lead to quarrels. When these conditions prevail the marriage is already on the rocks. It is useless as it is senseless to disregard the facts and to try foolishly to make the physical fact agree with the spiritual ideal. This is what people do who say the Bible grants no grounds for divorce save physical adultery alone. Jesus allows divorce on the grounds of fornication, for the simple reason that fornication is itself the process of divorce. The spiritual world always governs. As a man thinketh in his heart so is he. This is the Law. Fornication is thinking and feeling outside the Law, without understanding or observance of these truths. Therefore fornication is unlawful mental and emotional intercourse with ideas and concepts of delusion and darkness.

Let each marriage partner work within himself with the Great Law, claiming through God and by God the satisfaction of every true desire. Claiming health and happiness and beauty. Claiming that God is governing him wholly and entirely and that therefore he is under the beneficent compulsion to think and speak and act correctly. Let this give him peace and joy deep within himself. And then let him offer this peace and this joy as his gift to the marriage partner. This is love, the fulfilling of the law. It is the ideal of all people and it is practical and possible for you now.

Pay for what you want

THOU SHALT NOT STEAL

To STEAL IS TO ADMIT that you do not have. To steal is to deny God, deny his Great Law, deny yourself, and to enthrone the principle of limitation in your life. Everything you admit in your mind becomes a tendency toward action. Tendencies may become laws. To admit in the mind that stealing is a possible way of getting ahead is the real error rather than the act of stealing itself. A child may steal, but we attach no blame to the act even though we have to correct the child, for we understand that the child mind has not yet distinguished between good and evil in this world. The child mind is still very much in that heavenly state which sees no distinction between good and evil. The child responds to an instinct which tells it that all things were made for its joy and that anything it wants it can have. But the child has not yet learned that while you can have anything you want in this world, you must possess it by and through the Great Law of God and not by means of the first impulsive judgment of the senses. It is not wise to try to pet "the pretty kitty" of the woods. The child must learn to know the difference between the skunk of the woods and the house cat. The child, Emmanuel, the Bible says, shall eat butter and honey that he may know to refuse the evil and choose the good.

To reason and choose between good and evil is the business of this life, and the highest reasoning is that which is based upon the knowledge of the spiritual law. "Zion shall be redeemed with judgment . . ." (Isaiah 1:27) Everything in this world is under the spell of limitation and must be redeemed by spiritual wisdom. The instinctive life speaks truly: this is God's world and everything in it is beautiful. But man does not find it so until he knows the spiritual truth. Then his eyes are open. The instinctive life says that everything is good and that we may possess everything that our heart desires. The spell of the senses denies this. Yet the spell of the senses is an illusion and can be broken. Spiritual truth breaks this illusion. This Truth is called in the Bible the Redeemer of the world. Jesus has redeemed all who believe in him. Every innocent impulse, every passionate longing of the soul, must be redeemed with knowledge and right action. The soul is always right, but there is a way in which it is right and the mind must know that way.

Everything and anything that you want in this life is yours through the law of consciousness. That means that if you become conscious of possessing it you will have it. Everything you want exists now, right here, under a spell of disbelief or denial. It is this negative attitude which must be overcome in your mind. As you enlarge the field of your awareness you redeem the thing you want from darkness. You will always demonstrate or experience your awareness. All things are yours therefore, "and ye are Christ's, and Christ is God's." (I Corinthians 3:23) To be Christ's is to be a practitioner of the Great Law and to measure every wish and want, every process of the mind and every act of the hand, by your knowledge of the law of consciousness. Therefore, for you, it is never possible even to admit that stealing is a way to get ahead, for in your understanding you will see that stealing from another is really stealing from yourself. The emotion that prompts a man to steal, or even think of it, denotes a state of limitation which in itself will lead to loss. As Talbot Mundy points out, while you may never have stolen in your life, the question is, would you, if you had the chance? The tendency is enough to bring about loss in your affairs.

This explains why so many good people (good, in the world's definition of good) are often beset by limitations and defeats. Thieves break through and steal their possessions, bad business deals rob them of their substance and in many ways they seem to lose out to imposters and cheaters. They will protest that they never robbed anybody, why should someone rob them? But, as Talbot Mundy once said, you may not have robbed anyone, but would you, if you had the chance? That is the crux of the matter. If your policy is always to try to get something for nothing, then you have still to learn that you keep what you give. If you give nothing, nothing is what you keep. The Golden Rule, we read, is the fulfilling of the law, or it is the net result or the end product of observing the law in your own thought. The Golden Rule simply means that in your inmost thought and feeling you grant to every person upon the face of the earth his right to health and happiness and progression. Whatever you claim for yourself is also due every other son of God. If in your heart you do not grant this right of possession to another, but you withhold it through fear or jealousy or anger, then what you should learn and learn immediately is that in thus withholding it from another you are actually withholding it from yourself. You are the rust which is corrupting your possessions. And you are your own thief who is breaking through in the darkness of your own night and stealing your possessions.

Thou shalt not steal is a prohibition for the child-mind, which works to good ends. But for the enlightened mind the prohibition is unnecessary, for the words of the Commandment are merely a reminder of the law of consciousness and the way of prayer. If you pray daily by reiterating in your mind your knowledge of the Great Law, that you hold all things in consciousness, that the security of your possessions rests in the invisible hands of God which are stronger than the strongest banks and vaults in this world, then thieves will not molest the things that you own. When men know the real law and do not believe in lack or loss, there will be no thieves. For thieves are the verifications of your beliefs of limitation.

> Rob not the poor, because he is poor: neither oppress the afflicted in the gate: for the Lord will plead their cause, and spoil the soul of those that spoiled them. (Proverbs 22:22-23)

The temptation to get something for nothing is always with us and that is why we must be diligent to invoke the Great Prayer that we be led not into temptation. If our neighbor has left the gate open shall we take what attracts us? This would be childish, for it is self-thievery. For every such act of the hand there is a corresponding action in the mind. The thief does not believe in himself, in God or in the law. In his act of stealing he denies the very force in himself which alone can help him. Thus every outward gain of this kind is balanced by an inward loss. These inward losses or denials will eventually add up. Thus, the Lord will always plead the cause of the poor and spoil the soul of those that spoiled them. You will avoid the temptation to make an easy gain at the expense of someone else if you will remember that first of all the poor exist within you. Jesus says, "For ye have the poor always with you; but me ye have not always." (Matthew 26:11) And in Deuteronomy we read: "For the poor shall never cease out of the land: therefore I command thee, saying, Thou shalt open thine hand wide unto thy brother, to thy poor, and to thy needy, in the land." (Deuteronomy 15:11)

In your mental land, the poor and needy are the things you lack within, which prompt your wanting and desiring, and which initiate all progress in your life. For that reason it is said that the poor are blessed and that the kingdom of heaven is theirs. For that which is lowly may rise and that which is empty may be filled. The mind that is teachable may learn, but that which is full can receive no more. The mind that is satisfied can make no more progress. So give to these poor states in yourself. Give the stuff of life to them that they may be full and that you may make progress. The poor we have always with us because some limitation attends every state and condition in the relative world. Nothing that you can think of in this life is complete and finished. Everything can be improved. Everything is in a process of growing. Only in the spiritual world are things finished and complete. By daily meditation upon the law, by daily endeavoring in your thought to accept more health, more success, more happiness and more general beauty in your life, you feed the poor or limited states of mind. By such a process of meditation, which is really prayer or self-treatment, you establish in respect to any condition what we call the Christ-consciousness or the consciousness of fulness and redemption. It is this consciousness that is not always with you. You attain it in respect to one condition or another, but not in respect to all things at once. Our satisfactions with ourselves are not constant. After a job well done we are very pleased, but this satisfied feeling must eventually depart when we meet another challenge, another obstacle, have another immediate goal to strive for. In this way we continually make progress. So it is with the Christ-consciousness which also is not constantly with us but will assuredly come again after prayer and right thinking.

Thou shalt not steal is really a warning against greed—one of the seven deadly sins—and, conversely, in its positive sense, a prescription to the mind to think constructively. Greed is self-consumption and therefore the same as stealing from one's self. All excessive desires are thieving affirmations of lack, and of them the Christ-consciousness says, "All that ever came before me are thieves and robbers." (John 10:8) *meet opposition with facts*

THOU SHALT NOT BEAR FALSE WITNESS AGAINST THY NEIGHBOUR

THE HUMAN MIND IS LIKE A COURT OF LAW where a judge and jury sit listening to the evidence of two opposing sides. Every turning point in your life is a time of decision and judgment. These turning points may range anywhere from a simple rising from your chair to go into the other room to beginning an entirely new career. At every such time of decision you are listening to two sets of counsel.

There are two lawyers in your courtroom presenting evidence, each for his particular side. There is an urge or an ideal which pulls you forward, which bids you risk and plunge into some new activity. Opposed to this there are facts and circumstances, doubts, hesitancy, even fear itself, which bid you let well-enough alone. Like the Roman God, Janus, we all have two faces: one faces inward, toward God or the subjective world, and the other faces outward, toward conditions or the objective world. All of our lives we hear these two voices between judg-ments. And the inability of an individual to harmonize these two is the cause of all sickness and trouble. The voice of the inner world urges us forward to do and to be and to have. The voice of the outer world says be careful, watch out, you cannot, because circumstances will not let you.

A problem always indicates that these two sides are quarreling and overwhelming the judgment with words. In the heat and welter of the problem the mind often gets lost and for a time cannot find its way, until by resolute act of the will it begins to discriminate, to weigh and to judge. Then it is the cool of the day and we hear the voice of God calling to us in our garden and asking us, "Adam, what hast thou done?"

This is what we have done. We have listened to a voice from the land of the senses which has tried to accuse us, prosecute us and condemn us to some prison of sickness or defeat. It has come first of all whispering to us, casting a spell upon the mind which is innocent and devoid of the capacity to reason clearly about these things. Then the voice grows more bold and becomes a voluble browbeater. It may masquerade as religion and accuse the individual of being a terrible sinner, of having displeased God and wronged man. It plunges the individual into woeful feel-ings of inferiority and self-condemnation, self-pity, remorse and regret. Or, at times, of course, it may take an opposite

course and inflate the individual ego with feelings of su-
periority and pride and self-righteousness.

In every case it is the destroyer, the devil, the liar. For
any voice that tells you that you were not made for health,
for happiness and success in this life is a liar. Anything
that would stifle and stiffen the basic aspirations of your
being is the adversary, no matter what his appearance, to
whom God gave the dominion of the outermost sphere.

Yet one must not suppose that the devil is consummate
evil. These two poles of being which we are discussing are
simply the manifest and the unmanifest. Both are necessary. Both are ministers of God and life. And that is why
the devil comes from a royal family, as Mark Twain points
out. He is a fallen angel, for all that is manifest has come
out of the unmanifest, and matter is slowed-down spirit.
The hosts of heaven are the thoughts of the mind, and the
legions of Satan are the sensations of matter. A problem
always indicates that you are the victim of some limiting
sensation, that the mind has accepted some inhibiting or
restraining influence from the manifest world. In problems of bodily sickness the individual is found to fear some
external influence or power, he knows not what. He believes that his body or some organ or function of the body
is in bondage to the air, or to water, or to some external
organism. In problems of business and affairs a person
gets to believing that circumstances are against him, or,
which is much the same thing, that he is not adequate to
the demands of the circumstances. Yet all the while a
man desires to be well, desires to move ahead and to be

successful and happy, and so the quarrel goes on between the desire and the fact. Spiritual science shows us how to resolve this quarrel and the Great Law gives us precise directions of what to do.

It says, Do not bear false witness against your neighbor. That is, do not think and speak destructively about your neighbor. Now the neighbor is anyone or anything that is close to you. It is easy, in a physical sense, to see that the one who lives across the barberry hedge next door is your neighbor or the person you hear occasionally beyond the wall in your apartment. But you have a neighbor closer than these and that is the neighbor within your own mind. Whatever you are aware of as existing next to you, so to speak, but not yet one with you, is your neighbor. What concerns you most, what you think most often about, what floats into the immediate area of your awareness most often, this is your neighbor. As with neighbors in the outside world, so with this. You may be on good terms with him or you may be quarreling with him. It may be that it is some desire or project or enterprise that possesses your attention and is therefore the neighbor dwelling close to you. Every desire or hope or urge or will for expansion is really a visitor from heaven and should always be treated cordially. The vagrant wish should not be idly tossed from the mind. "Be not forgetful to entertain strangers," says Paul, "for thereby some have entertained angels unawares." (Hebrews 13:2) Every hope, inspiration and aspiration should be received cordially and enthusiastically. It should be met with food and raiment and shelter. That

is, a response of faith and belief on your part in the possibility of its embodiment and expression. If you believe
that thoughts are things, you will never turn away from
your door any inspiration which comes to it. In Christian
literature there are many stories which deal with this
point. One from Tolstoy is typical.

A poor cobbler befriends a stranger left naked in the
snow by robbers. He takes him home to his crude dwelling and teaches him the trade. At first the wife is out-
raged; then she, too, takes pity upon the stranger and feeds
and clothes him. The story unfolds with the stranger becoming a master shoemaker and the family's fortunes are
blessed. In the end of the tale the cobbler and his wife
discover, when the stranger takes his departure, that it is
none other than Michael, the archangel, who had been
living with them.

It is the word of God coming to the human mind which
is constantly being made flesh through faith. This is the
miracle of miracles. No one knows how it is done. But
anyone, through understanding, can partake more whole-
somely of the mystery. When the word of hope and promise comes to your mind, do not turn it away, do not
respond with some cynical or skeptical reply in thought or
in word. Do not say to yourself, "Oh, that is too good to
be true!" And do not say, "It is too late." Do not condition the word that comes to you with any limitation or
negation. Do not let your fear or anxiety strangle that
promise of God which comes to your mind. Rather meet it

with open arms of faith. Welcome it into your mind. Believe that there is a way for God to do what he promises to do in your life. Though all appearances suggest the contrary, still say to yourself, "There is nothing that is too good to be true, nothing too wonderful to happen to me and nothing too lovely to last." Welcome the Holy Visitor and he will do you good. Do not try to rely on your human wisdom, and try to devise ways and means of bringing about the good which the Visitor promises. Concentrate on the end; leave the means to God.

Receptiveness, agreement and acceptance—these are the first acts of the mind in such an instance. Welcome the Holy Visitor with these attitudes and do not try to make him obey your commands. For example, if the wish of your mind is to be delivered from the torments of an ugly person in your life, do not insist that the only way your problem can be solved is for your tormentor to be hurt or killed. God has many ways of solving any problem and he may conceivably solve your problem by making you love your tormentor. That would be a solution to your problem. If you want to be healed of a bodily ailment, the desire in your heart is the promise of God saying that you can be healed. But do not predicate your healing upon some special mode of treatment or upon a single form of therapy or upon some particular situation or environment. Accept the promise as it is given without any strings attached. Keep your faith in the end result without any qualification whatsoever. "Add thou not unto his words,

lest he reprove thee, and thou be found a liar," says Solomon. (Proverbs 30:6) Man's wisdom is foolishness with
God and one should guard against imposing his own ideas
upon the divine messengers.

Now we have considered the neighbor in your mind
from the standpoint of his angelic presence—the desire
and the aspiration which occupy your attention and therefore are the things closest to you. But, as in the outer
world, neighbors are good or bad and we are often in good
or bad relationships with them. So in the mind a neighbor
may appear as an inferior presence, or as an abhorrent and
an offensive state of mind. Whatever occupies your attention in fear or anxiety is also your neighbor, for it is that
of which you are most often aware, with which you hold
conversation frequently. In regard to this, the prescription
of the Ninth Word holds true: Do not bear false witness
against your neighbor. Even though you are scared to
death, do not allow your mind once to admit that the
thing you fear portends destruction or failure or anything
but momentary suffering. This negative presence in your
mind is only the opposite side of a single coin, the other
side of which we have just previously considered. The
coin is pure gold and it will buy life and all of its qualities and attributes in the market place. If in your game of
life your tossed coin has come up tails, and you frown in
disappointment, do not despair for another toss may show
heads up and you win. With this attitude you will always
have your generous share of the winnings and your losing
times will not hurt.

So do not bear false witness against that negative presence in your mind who is your neighbor. Whenever your mind is in a quandary or whenever you suffer from any limitation, this negative presence is in the mind alongside your positive desire.

If we return to the analogy of the courtroom for a moment, then we must say in relation to these two that the negative presence must die and the angelic presence live in your mind after prayer. Prayer is like the courtroom scene in which you build up evidence for the truth, for the positive impulse in your mind, and prove that the negative presence is a liar and guilty of destroying life. If, in your meditation, you become convinced that the fear or anxiety is groundless because there is no external power and that you were deluded in ascribing power to any external thing; and if, on the other hand, you do at the same time ascribe all power to the Word of God in your consciousness, believing that it has the mechanics and the mathematics of its own expression and that it can and will do all things necessary and implicit in its promise, then you have succeeded in what we call scientific prayer and have handed down a decision in the courtroom of your mind and sustained the positive good which has appeared there. You have condemned the guilty and set free the one who was falsely accused. This all comes from bearing true witness and giving proper evidence in the courtroom of your mind's deliberations.

To return now to the coin analogy we must see that

these two presences in the mind, faith and fear, are two parts of a single whole, and to bear true witness or give true testimony, we cannot destroy either one or the other but see each for what it is in itself and how they exist together for the progress of life. All fear is not bad; no more is all suffering or pain. When we are slothful in our praying and do not give enough attention to the positive values of life, some kind of pain or discomfort will always come in order to make us ask why and to inquire after wisdom. The negative presence in the mind is called the Denier because he denies or hides the positive value which is necessary for our growth. The negative is never a power in itself. It is a denial of power. When you feel low and inferior or sick and devitalized, it is not because some agency outside of yourself has robbed you of your life. Do not think such a thought and thus bear false testimony against this feeling of inadequacy in your mind. Rather regard your lowliness as subnormal realization and a minimum usage of your own inherent powers. The God-power is mind and consciousness, not forms and expressions. As you come to grips with these truths in your meditation, you will joyfully discover that what you thought were two quarreling opposites in your consciousness were really only two phases of consciousness, both signifying the same thing. Your fear is the darkness which hides the angel of your healing and promotion, and energizes you to seek that angel.

To bear true witness toward your neighbor, then, is to

meet every fear boldly and courageously, see it and understand it for what it is and do not give way to fearing fear
itself. Bearing true witness is also to acknowledge the
hope in your heart as divine and pregnant with immediate
possibilities of good.

CHAPTER TEN

Ignoring source causes envy

**THOU SHALT NOT COVET THY NEIGH-
BOUR'S HOUSE, THOU SHALT NOT COVET
THY NEIGHBOUR'S WIFE, NOR HIS MAN-
SERVANT, NOR HIS MAIDSERVANT, NOR
HIS OX, NOR HIS ASS, NOR ANY THING
THAT IS THY NEIGHBOUR'S**

THE OLD TESTAMENT GIVES THE LAW of human existence. The New Testament describes the fulfilling of that
law. The personification of that fulfillment says this: "If
I had not come and spoken unto them, they had not had
sin." (John 15:22) Jesus represents and portrays human
life when lived by the divine law. He is, therefore, the
embodiment of all of the ideals of humankind. Here, as
Emerson says, was a man who was true to what is in you
and me. The Christ man or God-self is called Emmanuel
by Isaiah, or God with us. It is the reality of every soul. The
average person recognizes this idealized version of himself
only in ideals, wishes, desires, and in the vague upward
reaches and yearnings of his being. Yet it is the very ideals

of the mind which cause its sin or its suffering. For if you had no ideal you would be satisfied with your present condition. A straw pallet in the corner would satisfy you if you had never known a better bed. But once discover that there are such things as better beds and you will want to try one and to own one. This is the way man makes progress, but it is also the way he suffers. You were content until you knew that there was something better. Desire brings pain, for it announces lack and limitation. "If I had not come and spoken unto them, they had not had sin." The sight of the ideal or a desire, or even a slight wish for betterment, plunges the consciousness into the state called sin. For it sets up a new mark of attainment, and the mind and body will suffer until that attainment is reached. That is why sin is defined as missing the mark. Jesus represents the mark and the prize in the high calling of every human life.

So here is the paradox: Desire is the mainspring of life. Without it, you will never move from where you are. It is the beginning of all progress and the foundation of all action. Yet desire is sin, for it announces lack and limitation and pain. The thoughtful reader will now see why sin has always been connected with human generation and also why so much of this kind of thinking was illusion and ignorance.

Every new state of things, whether in your life or in the society in which you live, was born out of desire, out of pain and suffering and the passion for betterment. But it is overloading the cart to say that your mother committed a sin in giving you birth. "In sin did my mother conceive me," was not spoken of the body but of the mind. Every one of us is born into this world in a state of ignorance and unreasoning. We do not know who we are nor what we are. We strive and fight for our place in the sun. We reach out eager hands for fruit on the tree of life, not knowing that some of it is green, some of it is poisonous, some of it hides venomous things. We know no way to distinguish nor to select what is good for us. This is the state called sin, because it is continuous desire without proper satisfaction.

And that is why the Tenth Word advises you not to covet, for covetousness is the sin we have just been describing. It is an error in thinking and feeling which prevents all health and happiness. For he who envies is emphasizing his own lack and limitation. He is affirming that he does not have, that he is empty and bereft, that other men possess the good things of life and he is without the pleasure that other men enjoy. The silent hearer within his consciousness records all of these affirmations and builds them up into failure and poverty and destruction.

The law is your thinking and your feeling. The law is consciousness. The law is belief. The person who covets has, by his covetous thinking and feeling, established a law of bondage for himself. The law is either freedom or bondage according to the way we relate ourselves to it, freedom or bondage to us according to our own acts. The criminal who robs a bank is putting himself under the penalty of a law which is set up for the protection of everybody's money including the criminal's. The law was made for freedom. "But I am carnal, sold under sin," as Paul says. (Romans 7:14) That is, I am sense-minded, given to looking at the surface of things, the forms of things, rather than the mind of things, and thereby I am sold into the bondage of my own illusions. All that is needed at any moment to deliver one is that one repent—think again, turn from negative, downward thinking to claim the reality of the ideal that shines before the mind.

Since consciousness is the law and thinking makes consciousness, then thinking upon health and strength and beauty without the acknowledgment of any other power to refute or distort your thinking, is to bring the conditions and relations of health and strength and beauty into embodiment and function in your individual life. But thinking about health and strength and beauty is a general form of mental action or prayer. You should also pray for those special, personal desires of yours which seem right and reasonable to you. Of course you cannot always tell what is right for you, but there are two ways to find out. First you can boldly claim every desire which comes to your mind, accept it, believe in it and pray it into reality and experience. Then when you get your desire, you may discover that it is not what you wanted at all. You may discover that it brought you harm instead of good. For example, a young man starts out in life with the thought that money can buy everything. He says to himself, I'm going to get money, come what may. With such determination, boldness and single-minded application, he does indeed win wealth. But in many cases he loses life. He becomes rough, calloused, headstrong and self-willed. He loses beauty out of his life and man cannot live without beauty. This fact made one of our early Colonial writers say, "I have somewhere met with a fable that made wealth the father of Love." It takes some people a long time of wealth-gathering in the material sphere before they discover that they have not acquired what they really wanted. But they have acquired wisdom in the process. They know now the difference between good and evil, between good desire and limiting desire. So there is some gain. I say you can use this method and get what you want (think you want) in life. But it is a long way around. It is a trial and error method. Because it is the method most frequently used by human beings, most people have to live all their lives before they understand what good things they should have desired. In a varying degree this is true of all of us. This life is a school and at its end we arrive at some wisdom. Thus we hear men and women of mature years saying, "If I had my life to live over again, I would . . ."

The other way of dealing with your desires and getting what you want is to pray for guidance. Admit that you do not know clearly what things will bring you real happiness. Pray for direction from the Deep Mind that does know. Formulate an over-all picture of the ideal life as it seems to you, composed of health, wealth, happiness, activity, beauty, love, peace and so forth. Let this be your main objective. If you believe that God's will for you is all of these qualities and conditions and much more besides, then you can shorten the whole definition of your objective into some such phrasing as "I want God's will in my life" or "I want the Divine Way and Plan in all my ways." Recall that the mind works like a syllogism. The major premise determines the conclusion the mind comes to in regard to any particular point or problem of concern to the mind. For example, an ordinary syllogism is this:

All material things change and pass away;
The Empire State Building is a material thing;
Therefore the Empire State Building will pass away.

The first statement is called the major premise. If your mind accepts the first statement and rests in it as a truth, then each time your mind considers any material thing it can come to only one conclusion about the final end and destiny of that thing. The conclusion will be in conformity with your major premise. The astute mental scientist will see that this is nothing more than what Jesus points out so clearly in the simple statement that "as thou hast believed, so be it done unto thee." (Matthew 8:13) Your major belief governs all your thinking, willing and doing. You get what you believe, you act as you believe. Your dominant devotion controls your life.

Therefore, if the major premise in your thinking is that God's will is the best and highest of all things good for you personally, on the mental, the spiritual and the material planes, then whenever and wherever you deal with any desire, undertaking or plan, your mind will automati-

cally protect you from false starts, unwise judgments, fruitless efforts and inefficient expenditure of energy in pursuits
that cannot bring you the real gold you are seeking.

But do not pray for guidance so much and so long that
you spend your time in indecision. We have no time to
learn all of the rules of life before we get into the game.
So attend to the things that are at hand. Deal with the
everyday desires that come to your mind. Do not stop to
wonder if God wants you to go into business, change jobs
or to be healthy. If you wish to help another who is ill,
don't meddle around with the dark thought that perhaps
God wants that person to die. Deal positively and vigor-
ously with every desire that seems good to you. Rely on
your major premise to aid you in making distinctions.
Your major premise is the Law. Realize that the Law is
governing all your thinking and doing. In other words
accept the fact of guidance, because by the immutable law
of mind you are being guided by your major premise.
With such guidance you will be able to distinguish between true desire and false desire, between those desires
which will promote your life and those which will merely
delay your happiness. Beware of the sin of indecision. A
double-minded man can expect nothing of the Lord or the
Law, for the state of his consciousness is like that of the
irresistible force meeting an immovable object. If you
desire to do right, to harm no one, and keep praying for
the guidance to know better what to do and what not to
do in your search for happiness, then move ahead with
your desires, welcome them into life, accept them all as

they come. Refuse no good that comes to you from the
hand of God. Everything that you desire is really a gift
from God being offered to you. Because you do not realize its possession, you feel the lack of it and interpret this
gift as a desire or a longing. This is much in the same way
as a baby in the crib is quiet and contented until it sees a
bright object on mother's dress, or a wrist watch on
father's hand. And immediately it desires it and reaches
eagerly for it. If there were nothing to desire we should
never desire. But it is precisely because the gifts of life,
in their spiritual state, are continually streaming toward
us that we reach out in aspiration and in longing. But
this longing, while it is a necessary beginning, is evil if it
be prolonged. Observe the Tenth Word: Do not envy
your neighbor's material wealth. Do not covet anything
and thereby deny it to yourself. Accept the spiritual states
which you desire and believe in them as reality now. Keep
on believing this until they become alive and functioning
in your objective world.

JESUS AND THE TEN COMMANDMENTS

J ESUS RESTATED THE TEN COMMANDMENTS in positive and simplified form. He did away with the Thou Shalt Nots and placed emphasis upon the personal affirmation of truth. He did this obviously upon the basis that it is much healthier to act than to refrain from acting, to seek safety than to run from danger, to work for the right rather than to oppose the wrong. Jesus everywhere emphasized the positive movement of life's force and warned against the worship of the false god of fear. Jesus teaches you to focus your attention upon what you want rather than to allow your consciousness to be absorbed with fear or guilt. If you see the Bible, as many people do, as a schematic representation of the spiritual life, then you will understand that the New Testament represents an age in mankind or a period in every man's life when the Christ-truth sits enthroned regnant and active on the personal plane. Such a time in the life of any individual is spiritual adulthood.

Therefore, Jesus treats the Ten Commandments from an adult point of view. As children we are given don'ts and shall nots to keep us in line, for being without understanding we are unable to think in terms of principles. With the coming of maturity we are shown the logic and wisdom behind these prohibitions. Then, instead of living under the stricture of other men's rules we live by our wisdom or by the law of our own understanding.

The Christ-consciousness is a law unto itself. This may be understood again by comparison with the civil law. Those laws of the land passed by the legislative bodies which prohibit stealing and killing and perjury and bigamy and so forth, are all the shall nots which are designed to hold the children of the race in line. But they are not perfect and so they do not work perfectly. There is no power to enforce these laws perfectly. There is no tribunal of man anywhere upon the earth which can force a single individual to do what his consciousness has not ordained him to do, and there never has been and never will be any tribunal of men which can force an individual man to refrain from doing what his consciousness is bent upon doing. This shows again the supremacy of that spiritual law inherent in man. The average man is still a child as regards this law, so he must live by representations of it, by facsimiles, by substitutes. When he is spiritually mature, however, he does not need these substitutes. He is his own righteous law from within and he is always moving toward righteous action. In an ideal world where every individual knew the law of consciousness and claimed his good from within and rejected error, no one could hurt another. If you coveted my ox you would become a victim of your own mind. Since you could not take the ox from my mental possession, the force you sent out in envy and attempted thievery could not manifest itself to me who had the consciousness of possession. It therefore would return to you, like the boomerang of the Australian bushman, and claim your ox or its equivalent in penalty.

There is an old teaching in the East as regards this point which is utterly and scientifically true today. It is that whatever spirit you invoke, good or bad, will not return to the invisible realm until it has accomplished its mission. One must make sure, therefore, always to invoke the spirits of good within himself.

While this ideal world we have just suggested does not exist universally today, any individual who sees the Great Law, understands it and puts it into practice by trusting to its government in his life, may live more in this ideal world irrespective of the condition of society about him. There are such individuals alive in the world today. They are many. They are the pillars and the supports of our social life. Without them, civilization would decay and sink into ruins. They are the giants who mold our age. There have always been such individuals and there always will be. The Bible calls them the elect. If you, by true spiritual practice, add yourself to their number, you make a real contribution to the stability and the peace of the world. For when their number increases all goes well.

When their number decreases the Four Horsemen ride across the earth.

Jesus said, "I came not to destroy the law, but to fulfil it." This is in conformity with the whole of the New Testament teaching. The Old Testament is the left-hand tablet, giving the law, the principle, the understanding of God. The New Testament is the right-hand tablet, fulfilling that law, putting that principle into practice and translating that understanding into human action. The Old Testament centers around several great characters, the New Testament around one. The Old Testament is impersonal and general. The New Testament is personal and specific. It relates entirely to God-action in the individual upon the personal plane. The Old Testament deals with the hidden being of God, the New Testament with the revealed being. The Christ is the revealer, interpreter and exemplifier of the hidden being of God. He is the word made flesh, the utterance, the expression, the particularization of the universal.

Indeed, one may say that Jesus, as the chief character of the New Testament, is the adult revision of the law and its progression to its fulfillment. As all utterance proceeds from hidden thought, visible forms from invisible principles, so the destiny of the unseen God of the world is to manifest himself in the form and shape of a perfect man. The perfect man would be one who had seen his source, understood that source and therefore his own nature and had put his understanding into practice. He would see

that the law of life on all planes is action and reaction; that
there is something which works and something which is
worked upon; that as the ancients said, God is one, but for
the purposes of creation He divides himself into two. A
man of spiritual comprehension sees that in himself these
two are what have been called the objective and subjective
minds; that there is something in him which thinks and
something which responds to thought. This responding
medium extends beyond his own human nature and acts as
though it were co-existent and co-extensive with the universe itself. Every thought one thinks awakes some emotional reaction, known or unknown. Repeated, persistent
thought in one direction builds up the emotional waters
that either destroy or become the rain that fructifies the
land of one's life.

A student of spiritual science will see that all of this is
figured admirably in the structure of the Ten Commandments. He will see that the Ten Words are not really ten
but essentially two words repeated ten times. For when
the man of spiritual wisdom is asked what the Great Law
is, he answers in terms of two: "The first of all the commandments is," he says, "Hear, O Israel; the Lord our God
is one Lord: and thou shalt love the Lord thy God with
all thy heart, and with all thy soul, and with all thy mind,
and with all thy strength: this is the first Commandment.
And the second is like, namely this, Thou shalt love thy
neighbour as thyself. There is none other commandment
greater than these." (Mark 12:29-31) There is no com-

mandment greater, because these are the ten reduced to two. The first statement comprehends all that is taught in the first tablet of the Law. It says in brief that there is one power, one law and that man should see, recognize, comprehend and understand and be devoted above all things to that one power. The second statement focuses all the meaning of the second tablet's Five Words into a single sentence. Its name is action, personal action, divine-right action through the individual. The two together reflect the truth that the love of God by man is always expressed in and through the love of man for man. More particularly, recognition of and work with the one supreme principle by you as an individual will express itself in your life as happy and harmonious relationships with all of the things and beings and conditions in your life.

On these two commandments, continues Jesus, hang all the Law and the Prophets. These are the eternal two which are busy day and night throughout all of the world. This is not just philosophy; it is also science. But as philosophy I believe it will come closer than any other basis you have heretofore found, to explaining the phenomena of life. As science it is the basis of a sane, successful and beautiful life.

But creation does not stop with two. No more should our understanding of the Great Law. In every creative act and therefore in every regenerative motion, two forces are at work to produce a third. In this third the identity of the two parents is involved but lost in a new identity.

The desire in me to write this book was its father. The response my mind made in the discipline and labor necessary to produce it, was its mother. These two came together and produced the third which I am now beginning to see in form as I once saw it in desire. These two parents have finished their work. They are perishing, for I no longer have the desire to write a book, and discipline and labor in regard to this work are no longer necessary. The two have blended into a one. When I desired and labored I was in the Old Testament following Moses, the man of God, listening to the law, on my way to the Promised Land. Now with the book taking shape, I am in the New Testament day, seeing the actual visible form which was once evidenced to me only by faith. The Law and the Gospel are now one. The Gospel being the good news of what the Law has done.

I have drawn this personal illustration to illustrate the closing point of our discussion of the Great Law. We must now close the Book of the Covenant, so that instead of two tablets, two pages, we shall have but one, written on both sides, inside and without. When desire and faith mate and become one the result is unity, love, peace, joy and all the attributes of the God-head. That resulting one is the eternal One. It was no accident that the Great Law was written in ten parts. For this was purposely designed to show that the Law is one and Being is one.

As in the universal, so in the particular, the Law is the same. Mind is that One. In every creative act of man mind is the only actor and the law of mind is the supreme law. All things and processes are but the function and the portrayal of that one. Numbers are so. Numeration is but the adding of units in order to define and describe different conditions of phenomena. Numeration is the play and the festival of the one. The number one is alone and abides without any other. It arises out of darkness from zero and vanishes again into that nothingness of infinity. It begets all of the other numbers but is begotten by none of them. It is the maker of all conditions but is not made or qualified by any condition. This is the universal law, the principle of God himself, as we witness it in numbers. The number ten indicates that the one has moved, created and returned to rest.

It is the same in all creation. All the diversity of nature tells the same story—that it came from one and to one it will return. To reduce this principle once more to a practical consideration, observe again that in man this one is Mind, the divine element. Mind in man is the maker and the master of all of his life. It is the invisible playwright, producer, actor and witness of the whole drama of human life. Mind creates by dividing into two, desire and enthusiasm. These two come together and reproduce a third, which is the one at a higher level of expression. This higher level of expression is the triumph over pain, frustration, so-called enemies and all trouble. This regenerate one, dwelling above its former misery, does not project any fear, hate, resentment or enmity whatever into the

external world of people, animals, plants and things. It
is at one with itself and with all other forms of expression
everywhere. This is love, and love is the fulfilling of the
law.